Frommer's®

P9-DMK-112

London
day BY day™

2nd Edition

by Lesley Logan

WILEY

Wiley Publishing, Inc.

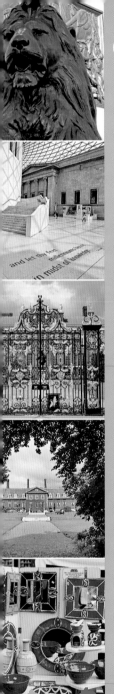

Contents

Published by:

Wiley Publishing, Inc.

111 River St.
Hoboken, NJ 07030-5774

ISBN 978-0-470-38226-4

Editor: Naomi P. Kraus
Production Editor: Katie Robinson
Photo Editor: Richard Fox
Cartographer: Andrew Murphy
Production by Wiley Indianapolis Composition Services

For information on our other products and services or to obtain technical support, please contact our Customer Care Department within the U.S. at 800/762-2974, outside the U.S. at 317/572-3993 or fax 317/572-4002.

Wiley also publishes its books in a variety of electronic formats. Some content that appears in print may not be available in electronic formats.

Manufactured in China

5   4   3

A Note from the Editorial Director

Organizing your time. That's what this guide is all about.

Other guides give you long lists of things to see and do and then expect you to fit the pieces together. The Day by Day guides are different. These guides tell you the best of everything, and then they show you how to see it *in the smartest, most time-efficient way*. Our authors have designed detailed itineraries organized by time, neighborhood, or special interest. And each tour comes with a bulleted map that takes you from stop to stop.

Hoping to relive the glory days of Merry Ole England, or tour the highlights of the British Museum? Planning a walk through Chelsea, or a whirlwind tour of the best that London has to offer? Whatever your interest or schedule, the Day by Days give you the smartest routes to follow. Not only do we take you to the top attractions, hotels, and restaurants, but we also help you access those special moments that locals get to experience—those "finds" that turn tourists into travelers.

The Day by Days are also your top choice if you're looking for one complete guide for all your travel needs. The best hotels and restaurants for every budget, the greatest shopping values, the wildest nightlife—it's all here.

Why should you trust our judgment? Because our authors personally visit each place they write about. They're an independent lot who say what they think and would never include places they wouldn't recommend to their best friends. They're also open to suggestions from readers. If you'd like to contact them, please send your comments our way at feedback@frommers.com, and we'll pass them on.

Enjoy your Day by Day guide—the most helpful travel companion you can buy. And have the trip of a lifetime.

Warm regards,

Kelly Regan

Kelly Regan, Editorial Director
Frommer's Travel Guides

About the Author

Lesley Logan is a writer, editor, and long-time resident of London, who has worked in publishing for over two decades and holds dual citizenship from the U.S. and the U.K. She is the author of several books, including *The Unofficial Guide to London.*

Acknowledgments

I would like to thank all my native Londoner friends who have inspired me with their loyalty to this outrageous, delightful city over the years, and who have taken me down paths I would not have found on my own. Thanks too, to all the shopkeepers, restaurateurs, curators, guides, hotel staff, neighbors, and strangers who have been so generous in offering their time and experiences. To Jacqueline Kispal, who did the hard work of having fun in clubs for this edition—brava! A special debt of gratitude goes to Naomi Kraus, editor extraordinaire. As always, my most heartfelt and deepest thanks belong to my husband Tom and my daughter Nora.

An Additional Note

Please be advised that travel information is subject to change at any time—and this is especially true of prices. We therefore suggest that you write or call ahead for confirmation when making your travel plans. The authors, editors, and publisher cannot be held responsible for the experiences of readers while traveling. Your safety is important to us, however, so we encourage you to stay alert and be aware of your surroundings.

Star Ratings, Icons & Abbreviations

Every hotel, restaurant, and attraction listing in this guide has been ranked for quality, value, service, amenities, and special features using a **star-rating system.** Hotels, restaurants, attractions, shopping, and nightlife are rated on a scale of zero stars (recommended) to three stars (exceptional). In addition to the star-rating system, we also use a **kids** icon to point out the best bets for families. Within each tour, we recommend cafes, bars, or restaurants where you can take a break. Each of these stops appears in a shaded box marked with a coffee-cup-shaped bullet ☕ .

The following **abbreviations** are used for credit cards:

AE	American Express	DISC	Discover	V	Visa
DC	Diners Club	MC	MasterCard		

Frommers.com

Now that you have this guidebook to help you plan a great trip, visit our website at **www.frommers.com** for additional travel information on more than 4,000 destinations. We update features regularly to give you instant access to the most current trip-planning information available. At Frommers.com, you'll find scoops on the best airfares, lodging rates, and car rental bargains. You can even book your travel online through our reliable travel booking partners. Other popular features include:

- Online updates of our most popular guidebooks
- Vacation sweepstakes and contest giveaways
- Newsletters highlighting the hottest travel trends
- Podcasts, interactive maps, and up-to-the-minute events listings
- Opinionated blog entries by Arthur Frommer himself
- Online travel message boards with featured travel discussions

A Note on Prices

In the "Take a Break" and "Best Bets" sections of this book, we have used a system of dollar signs to show a range of costs for 1 night in a hotel (the price of a double-occupancy room) or the cost of an entree at a restaurant. Use the following table to decipher the dollar signs:

Cost	Hotels	Restaurants
$	under $150	under $20
$$	$150–$250	$20–$30
$$$	$250–$350	$30–$40
$$$$	$350–$450	$40–$50
$$$$$	over $450	over $50

An Invitation to the Reader

In researching this book, we discovered many wonderful places—hotels, restaurants, shops, and more. We're sure you'll find others. Please tell us about them, so we can share the information with your fellow travelers in upcoming editions. If you were disappointed with a recommendation, we'd love to know that, too. Please write to:

Frommer's London Day by Day, 2nd Edition
Wiley Publishing, Inc. • 111 River St. • Hoboken, NJ 07030-5774

16 Favorite
Moments

16 Favorite **Moments**

1. Take photos from the top of the London Eye
2. Chat with Sir Walter Raleigh and other historical figures at the Tower of London
3. Eat ice cream at the intermission of a first-class production
4. Drink champagne and dig the music (classical or jazz) at the Late View at the V&A
5. Dine next to a celebrity at the Wolseley
6. Print a poster of your favorite masterpiece at the National Gallery
7. Crisscross the scenic Serpentine in a paddle boat
8. Finish a brass rubbing at St Martins-in-the-Field
9. Haggle for a bargain at Portobello Road Market
10. Listen to Big Ben strike the hour

Previous page: A nighttime view of the Palace of Westminster, one of London's most beautiful sights.

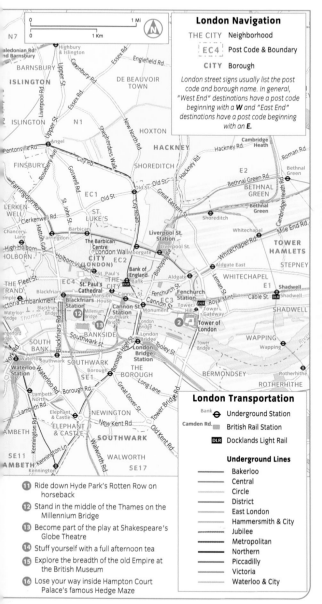

London Navigation

THE CITY   Neighborhood

EC4   Post Code & Boundary

CITY   Borough

*London street signs usually list the post code and borough name. In general, "West End" destinations have a post code beginning with a **W** and "East End" destinations have a post code beginning with an **E**.*

London Transportation

Bank ⊖   Underground Station

Camden Rd. ▪   British Rail Station

DLR   Docklands Light Rail

Underground Lines

——— Bakerloo
——— Central
——— Circle
——— District
——— East London
——— Hammersmith & City
——— Jubilee
——— Metropolitan
——— Northern
——— Piccadilly
——— Victoria
——— Waterloo & City

⓫ Ride down Hyde Park's Rotten Row on horseback

⓬ Stand in the middle of the Thames on the Millennium Bridge

⓭ Become part of the play at Shakespeare's Globe Theatre

⓮ Stuff yourself with a full afternoon tea

⓯ Explore the breadth of the old Empire at the British Museum

⓰ Lose your way inside Hampton Court Palace's famous Hedge Maze

"When a man is tired of London, he's tired of Life, for there is in London all that Life can afford." Dr. Samuel Johnson may have been exaggerating a bit, but boredom with London may indeed be a sign of depression. On the rare occasions I become weary of this marvelous city, the experiences outlined in this section are my mood-elevating prescriptions. Side effects may include euphoria, infatuation, and a sudden loss of pounds (sterling, that is).

① Take photos from the top of the London Eye. The top of this Ferris wheel is the best place to get a picture-perfect shot of London's far-reaching landscape. Any time is a good moment to take this "flight," but for a truly breathtaking photo op, jump aboard on a late afternoon as the sun starts sinking and the lights come on across the city. *See p 12, ⑦.*

② Chat with Sir Walter Raleigh, William the Conqueror, and other historical figures at the Tower of London. The Tower's entertaining actors have their characters' life stories down pat, and are walking, talking history. Don't be shy; they love to interact with visitors and answer questions. They may even approach you in a friendly, if archaic ("What ho, my good lady? Methinks thou art in need of a boon companion") manner as you wander around. *See p 16, ①.*

③ Eat ice cream at the intermission of a first-class production as a well-deserved splurge for having gotten a half-price ticket for a very good seat at one of London's many famous theaters. If ice cream's not your thing, order drinks before your play starts and pick them up during the "interval." *See p 134.*

④ Drink champagne and dig the music (classical or jazz) at the Late View at the V&A, held under the museum's thrilling Dale Chihuly glass chandelier on Friday evening. Several of the renowned museum's galleries are open for exploring, and the relaxed atmosphere makes for a leisurely and seductive visit. Pick up a ticket for one of the lectures that start at 7pm, and round out the night with a browse through the gift shop. *See p 26.*

⑤ Dine next to a celebrity at the Wolseley, but act unimpressed.

A pod on the British Airways London Eye.

Holbein's The Ambassadors *is just one of many National Gallery masterpieces.*

Don't even think about autographs, cameras, or gaping at this Piccadilly hot spot, where the modern British cuisine is good and the clientele often stellar. Make lunch and dinner reservations in advance of your visit. Weekdays and nights are better than weekends to catch sight of a celeb, and remember that only Americans dine before 8pm. *See p 108.*

⑥ Print a poster of your favorite masterpiece at the National Gallery. The computers in this world-renowned museum's Sainsbury Wing offer virtual reconnaissance tours of this huge, treasure-packed museum and allow you to browse, choose, and print out high-quality posters of your favorite paintings in a variety of sizes. The database is huge and intelligently organized—it's a real kick to scroll through. *See p 23, ⑦.*

⑦ Crisscross the scenic Serpentine in a paddle boat on a sunny morning as ducks and geese wheel overhead. The little island on the north side is reputed to be local resident J. M. Barrie's inspiration for the Island of the Lost Boys in *Peter Pan.* Bring a camera and your energy, or opt for a rowboat and let a companion do the work. *See p 88, ⑤.*

⑧ Finish a brass rubbing at St. Martin-in-the-Fields, an activity perfect for one of London's many rainy afternoons. There are dozens of beautiful brasses of different sizes and styles to choose from. The finished work makes a gorgeous (and relatively inexpensive) souvenir. It's a big hit with kids and crafty types. *See p 43, ④.*

⑨ Haggle for a bargain at Portobello Road Market, either at the open-air stalls or in the warrens of indoor arcades. You may get 10% to 15% off the asking price, which everyone involved knows is set just for that probability. Saturday's the big day for this famous antiques market, and part of the fun is sharing the street with seething crowds of bargain hunters and loiterers. *See p 83.*

⑩ Listen to Big Ben strike the hour, an event that thrills even Londoners. It's the bell itself that's named Big Ben, though most assign that name to the whole clock tower. Though the bell has a crack in it and can't sound an E note, its chimed aria from Handel's *Messiah* is the undisputed aural symbol of London. *See p 10, ②.*

Outdoor stalls at Portobello Road Market.

⓫ Ride down Hyde Park's Rotten Row on horseback and you'll feel like a character from a 19th-century English novel, as you pass joggers, in-line skaters, and bicyclists. There's no better way to absorb the atmosphere of London's most popular park. Only skilled riders should let their horses try a canter; novices will enjoy the experience most at a walking gait. *See p 87,* ③.

⓬ Stand in the middle of the Thames on the Millennium Bridge, which spans not just the river, but the centuries, with St. Paul's Cathedral on one side and the Tate Modern on the other. The views of the cityscape are impressive, especially at sunrise and sunset. *See p 13,* ❿.

⓭ Become part of the play at Shakespeare's Globe Theatre as one of the "groundlings" who stand in front of the stage, much as the rabble did during Shakespeare's time. You never know when the actors might mingle among you as they bellow out their lines. It's a truly Elizabethan experience, minus the thieves and the spitting. *See p 135.*

⓮ Stuff yourself with a full afternoon tea at one of the many deluxe hotels that rise to the task of impressing visitors with an array of tea sandwiches, scones, clotted cream, and

Riders trot down Hyde Park's Rotten Row.

A view of St. Paul's Cathedral from the Millennium Bridge.

desserts—all washed down with a strong cuppa. Make no dinner plans—you won't be hungry. *See p 94.*

⓯ Explore the breadth of the old Empire at the British Museum, where priceless treasures acquired from all parts of the globe—including the Rosetta Stone and the Elgin Marbles—testify to the power that Britain once exerted over the farthest reaches of the world, and give you insight into just how greedy its adventurers were. If your interests tend more toward the literary, there are few better places in the world to soak up the power of the written word than the museum's famous Reading Room. *See p 31.*

⓰ Lose your way inside Hampton Court Palace's famous Hedge Maze, whose winding paths cover nearly half a mile. When you manage to extricate yourself from its clutches, stroll through the many centuries of architectural styles featured at this stunning palace, which was the country home of many an English monarch. Don't neglect the gift shops. *See p 51,* ⑨. ●

The Best **in One Day**

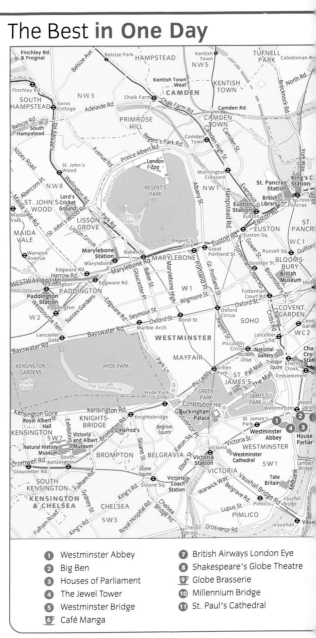

1	Westminster Abbey	**7**	British Airways London Eye
2	Big Ben	**8**	Shakespeare's Globe Theatre
3	Houses of Parliament	**9**	Globe Brasserie
4	The Jewel Tower	**10**	Millennium Bridge
5	Westminster Bridge	**11**	St. Paul's Cathedral
6	Café Manga		

Previous page: One of Trafalgar Square's famous lions.

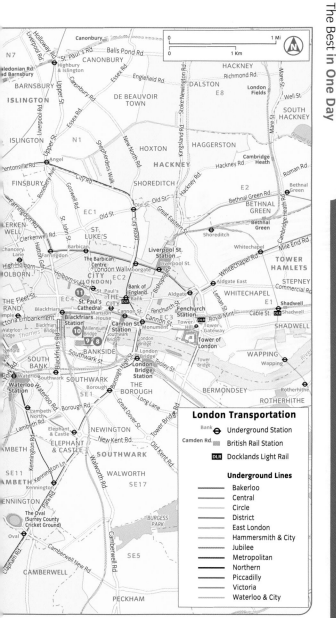

With London's abundance of sights, how much can you manage to see in just one day? Plenty. In this tour, you'll visit the oldest (Westminster Abbey); the newest (British Airways London Eye); and something that stands (time wise) in between: the painstakingly authentic reconstruction of Shakespeare's Globe Theatre. Throw in classic London cityscapes viewed from some of the famous bridges that span the Thames River, and you've got yourself a great 1-day jaunt that won't leave you feeling exhausted. START: **Westminster Tube Station**

1 ★★★ Westminster Abbey. Westminster Abbey is one of the finest examples of medieval architecture in Europe. Laid to rest here are the towering figures of English life. Some 3,300 memorials to kings, nobles, and an assortment of church worthies are here for the viewing. William the Conqueror, Edward III (who willed that his heart be removed before burial to rest with his mum's remains in Grey Friar's Church), Mary Queen of Scots, Elizabeth I (whose death mask was the model for her tomb's figure), and Henry V, the hero of Agincourt—all have elaborately decorated sarcophagi. Don't miss the Gothic ceilings (reflected in a large mirror for close-up viewing), the stained glass in the Chapter House, and the elaborate carvings of the Henry VIII Chapel's choir stalls. And make your way to Poet's Corner,

The Choir Apse at Westminster Abbey.

where you'll find monuments to well-loved literary names such as Chaucer, Austen, and Dickens. ⏱ *1½ hr.; arrive before 9:30am to avoid lines. 20 Dean's Yard.* ☎ *0207/222-5152. www.westminster-abbey.org. Admission £10 adults, £7 seniors & kids 11–16, £24 family, free for kids 10 & under; Free admission to services. Mon–Sat 9:30am–3:45pm; Closed Sun. Tube: Westminster.*

2 ★★★ Big Ben. The iconic Clock Tower at the eastern end of the Palace of Westminster has come to be known as Big Ben, though that appellation really refers to the largest bell in the clock's chime. The 14-ton bell, installed in 1858, is believed to have been named for

The name Big Ben actually refers to the bell in the famous clock's chime.

the commissioner of public works at the time—Sir Benjamin Charles—although some historians insist it was named for a famous boxer of the era, Benjamin Caunt. Brits can make the ascent up the tower's 334 spiral steps by special guided tour, but non-U.K. citizens must content themselves with a must-have snapshot. ⏲ *5 min. Near St. Stephen's Entrance of Westminster Palace, Old Palace Yard. British citizens should contact their local MP to apply for permission to tour the clock tower.*

The Palace of Westminster, home to both Houses of Parliament.

③ ★★ **Houses of Parliament.** The immense 3-hectare (7.4-acre) Palace of Westminster, a splendid example of Gothic Revival architecture, dates back to 1840 (the original palace was all but destroyed by fire in 1834). It's the home of the 659-member House of Commons (where elected officials do their legislating) and the 700-plus-member House of Lords (where they second-guess the decisions made in the Commons). You may observe debates for free from the Stranger's Galleries in both houses, but the long entry lines make this spot better for a quick photo op than a lengthy visit. The only exception: U.K. citizens can take worthwhile guided tours of the premises on select days throughout the year; non-U.K. citizens can take a guided tour only during Parliament's summer break. ⏲ *5 min. Old Palace Yard.* ☎ *0207/ 219-3000 House of Commons; 0207/219-3107 House of Lords. www. parliament.uk. Free admission. Mon–Wed 2:30–10:30pm; Thurs 11:30am–7:30pm; Fri 9:30am–3pm. Closed Easter week. Guided tours (£12 adults, £5 kids 16 & under) offered to non-U.K. residents July–Oct only*

(check website or call for exact tour times). Tube: Westminster.

④ ★ **The Jewel Tower.** This medieval structure was one of only two buildings to survive an 1834 fire that destroyed the original Palace of Westminster. The tower dates back to 1365 and was originally used to house Edward III's wardrobe and treasures. Today, it's home to a very informative exhibit, "Parliament Past & Present," which details the inner workings of the British government. Look carefully at the building's exterior as you enter and you'll spot the remains of a moat. ⏲ *25 min. Abingdon St.* ☎ *0207/222-2219. www. english-heritage.org.uk. Admission £2.90 adults, £1.50 kids 12 & under. Apr–Oct daily 10am–5pm; Nov–Mar daily 10am–4pm.*

⑤ **Westminster Bridge.** From the center of this bridge you can enjoy a sweeping view of the Houses of Parliament and Big Ben—one of the most familiar and beloved cityscapes in the world. ⏲ *10 min. Tube: Westminster.*

The medieval Jewel Tower was once the treasure house of Edward III.

6 ★ **Café Manga,** located in County Hall, also has outdoor seating behind the London Eye. It's a Japanese anime-themed joint, but don't let that put you off: They serve plenty of good food and drinks, and the people-watching opportunities are endless. *Westminster Bridge Rd.* ☎ *0207/928-5047. $.*

7 ★★★ **kids British Airways London Eye.** The huge Ferris wheel that solemnly rotates at one revolution per half-hour has quickly become a London icon. It graces the skyscape from as far away as Hyde Park, and is much loved by even the most hardened London traditionalists. Although it was originally planned for only a 5-year stint, there's no way the London Tourist Board will let it go. You are encouraged to buy your timed ticket well in advance, which can end up in disappointment if you get a gray and rainy day. You may, however, be able to buy same-day tickets during the off season, which can eliminate the guesswork about the weather. Show up 30 minutes before your scheduled departure time (15 if you have a Fast Track ticket). Don't forget your camera. ⏱ *1 hr., from lining up through half-hour ride. Book Fast Track tickets via the website or in person for double the price. Book through the website for a 10% discount. South Bank (at Westminster Bridge).* ☎ *0870/500-0600. www. londoneye.com. Admission £15 adults, £12 seniors, £7.50 kids 5–15, free for kids 4 & under.*

Sept–June daily 9:30am–8pm; July–Aug daily 9:30am–10pm. Closed bank holidays & 3 weeks in Jan. Tube: Westminster.

The British Airways London Eye offers some of the best views in London.

8 ★★★ **kids Shakespeare's Globe Theatre.** Even if you don't have tickets to a play (p 135), the Globe is a fascinating place to visit. It was rebuilt in painstaking detail on a parking lot near the site of the original theater (and only those tools authentic to the period of the original were used in its construction). It was at the Globe in the late 1500s/early 1600s that Shakespeare's comedies and tragedies were performed in daylight (as they are now) to delight the nobility (who sat in the tiers) as well as the rabble (who stood before the stage). You can choose either option when purchasing tickets, weighing comfort versus proximity to the stage. Changing exhibits focus on related topics such as the frost fairs of medieval London (back when the Thames would freeze into solid terrain, and people would party on the river for days); or the juicy history of nearby Southwark, once a haven for prostitutes, thieves,

Shakespeare's Globe Theatre is a perfect replica of the Bard's original.

and actors. ⏱ *1 hr. 21 New Globe Walk.* ☎ *0207/902-1500 (exhibition) or 0207/401-9919 (box office). www.shakespeares-globe.org. Admission to museum & exhibits: £9 adults, £7.50 seniors, £6.50 kids 5–15, £25 family (2 adults & 3 kids). Daily 10am–5pm (closed during afternoon theater matinees—call for schedules). Tube: London Bridge.*

The 🍴 ★★ kids **Globe Brasserie** is a fine choice for a restorative tea and sandwich, along with a Thames-side view of London. The menu features deliciously prepared English favorites, such as cottage pies, as well as more modern sandwiches and salads. *21 Globe Walk, SE1 (off Thames Path).* ☎ *0207/902-1576. $.*

⓾ ★★★ kids **Millennium Bridge.** This gorgeous sliver of a footbridge connecting Bankside to The City and its attractions is an efficient way to cross the river and a wonderful spot from which to take photos of the surrounding landmarks. When it first opened in 2000, it swayed and had to be shut down, but it has since been stabilized. ⏱ *10 min. Tube: Southwark or Blackfriars.*

⓫ ★★★ kids **St. Paul's Cathedral.** For centuries, the Dome of St. Paul's had no competition in the skyline of London; it was the

The ultramodern Millennium Bridge is one of the city's newest landmarks.

St. Paul's Cathedral, Sir Christopher Wren's crowning achievement.

highest and most impressive building in town. Though it has since been dwarfed by the skyscrapers in the financial district, none of them inspires the same awe as Sir Christopher Wren's masterpiece, built after the Great Fire of 1666. The cathedral is the culmination of Wren's unique and much-acclaimed fusion of classical (the exterior Greek-style columns) and baroque (the ornate interior decorations) architecture. The Whispering Gallery is a miracle of engineering, in which you can hear the murmurs of another person from across a large gallery. The 530 stairs to the top are demanding, but you'll be rewarded with a magnificent view, not only of London, but of the marvel of the cathedral, which Wren—who is buried alongside many notable scientists and artists in the church's crypt—considered his ultimate achievement and most demanding effort. There are guided tours at 11am, 11:30am, 1:30pm, and 2pm. ⏱ *½ hr. Ludgate Hill, EC4 (at Paternoster Sq.).* ☎ *0207/236-4128. www.stpauls.co. uk. Admission £10 adults, £9 seniors, £3.50 kids 15 & under. Mon–Sat 8:30am–4:30pm. Tube: St. Paul's.*

The Best **in Two Days**

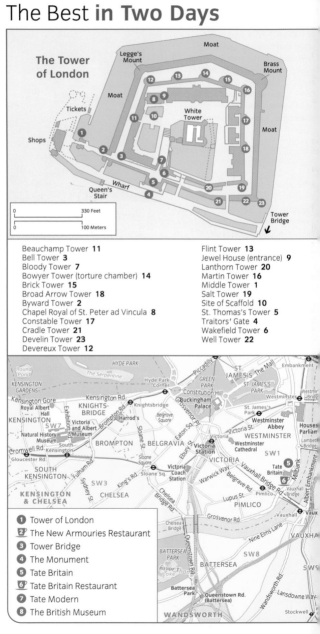

Beauchamp Tower **11**
Bell Tower **3**
Bloody Tower **7**
Bowyer Tower (torture chamber) **14**
Brick Tower **15**
Broad Arrow Tower **18**
Byward Tower **2**
Chapel Royal of St. Peter ad Vincula **8**
Constable Tower **17**
Cradle Tower **21**
Develin Tower **23**
Devereux Tower **12**

Flint Tower **13**
Jewel House (entrance) **9**
Lanthorn Tower **20**
Martin Tower **16**
Middle Tower **1**
Salt Tower **19**
Site of Scaffold **10**
St. Thomas's Tower **5**
Traitors' Gate **4**
Wakefield Tower **6**
Well Tower **22**

1 Tower of London
2 The New Armouries Restaurant
3 Tower Bridge
4 The Monument
5 Tate Britain
6 Tate Britain Restaurant
7 Tate Modern
8 The British Museum

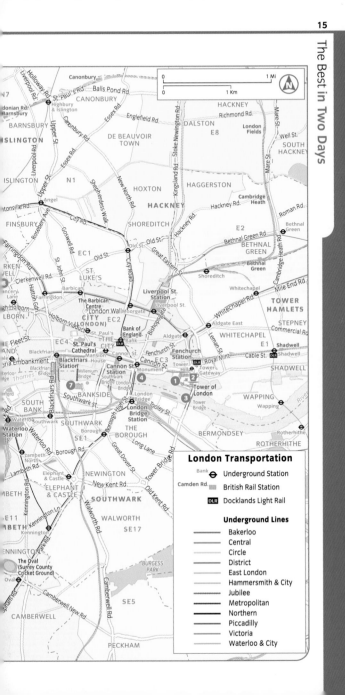

London Transportation

Bank   ⊖   Underground Station

Camden Rd.   ▢   British Rail Station

DLR   Docklands Light Rail

Underground Lines

———— Bakerloo
———— Central
———— Circle
———— District
———— East London
———— Hammersmith & City
———— Jubilee
———— Metropolitan
———— Northern
———— Piccadilly
———— Victoria
———— Waterloo & City

On your second day in London, you will circle the globe and leap across centuries without ever leaving the city precincts. Even blasé Londoners are excited by the cauldron of history that is the Tower of London, the spoils of the Empire at the British Museum, the view from the top of the Monument, and the iconoclastic art of the 20th and 21st centuries ensconced at the Tate Modern. And as a bonus, you get to traverse the Thames by boat. START: **Tower Hill Tube Station**

1 ★★★ kids **Tower of London.** Built by William the Conqueror in 1066, this fortress was added to by subsequent generations of kings and queens up to the Victorian Age, and is now an incomparable collection of buildings that reflect the range of England's architectural styles over the past millennium. The Tower has a bloody past marked by power struggles, executions, and cruelty: The young nephews of Richard III were murdered here in 1483; two of Henry VIII's six wives (Anne Boleyn and Catherine Howard) were beheaded on Tower Green, as was the 9-day queen, Lady Jane Grey; and Sir Walter Raleigh left his name on a walkway by his prison cell. Yeoman Warders (or "Beefeaters") give sprightly talks all day long, and talented actors offer living history lessons as they wander about in period costumes. The Crown Jewels are the most popular sight, just edging out the Torture Exhibit; the two together represent the awful accouterments of power (and have the longest lines). The Tower, quite justifiably regarded as one of the most haunted—and haunting—places in London, will thrill students of history, and entertain kids as well. ⏱ *3 hr. Buy your tickets online & arrive before 9am to avoid the long line & save a small amount of money, as well as time. Tower Hill.* ☎ *0870/756-6000. www.hrp. org.uk. Admission £16 adults, £13 seniors, £9.50 kids 5–15, free for*

The Imperial State Crown, one of England's famous Crown Jewels.

kids 4 & under. Open daily 9am– 6pm; till 5pm Nov–Feb. Tube: Tower Hill.

Buy take-away sandwiches and drinks at **2** ★★ **The New Armouries Restaurant** for an outdoor picnic, or settle in for a hot lunch of shepherd's pie, soup, Yorkshire pudding, or whatever you fancy. It's clean and pleasant though not hugely atmospheric. There are also snack shops scattered here and there around the Tower. *Inside the Tower of London.* ☎ *0870/756-6000. $.*

The Tower of London is actually a fortress encompassing many buildings.

Tower Ghosts

The Tower of London, said to be the most haunted spot in England, fairly overflows with supernatural manifestations of tormented souls.

One of the Tower of London's famous resident ravens.

The restless ghost of Queen Anne Boleyn (executed in 1536 on a trumped-up charge of treason after she'd failed to produce a male heir for Henry VIII) is the most frequently spotted spirit. The tragic shades of the Little Princes (the two sons of Edward IV)—allegedly murdered by Richard III in 1483—have been spied in the Bloody Tower. Ghostly reenactments of the Tower Green beheading of the Countess of Salisbury—who was hacked to death by her inept executioner on May 27, 1541—have been seen on its anniversary. The ghostly screams of Guy Fawkes, who gave up his co-conspirators in the Gunpowder Plot after suffering unspeakable torture, reputedly still echo around the grounds.

Other notable spirits you may encounter (the no-nonsense Tower guards have had run-ins with them all) include St. Thomas á Becket, Sir Walter Raleigh, Lady Jane Grey, and Henry VI.

❸ ★★ kids **Tower Bridge.** This picture-perfect bascule bridge—a term derived from the French for "seesaw"—has spanned the Thames since 1894. There's no denying the physical beauty of the neo-Gothic bridge: Its skeleton of steel girders is clothed with ornate masonry using Cornish granite and Portland stone designed to harmonize elegantly with the neighboring Tower of London. Its lower span opens and closes through hydraulics and behemoth machinery—details that even engineering-challenged visitors will find fascinating on the "Tower Bridge Experience" tour. Tour participants can also ascend to the bridge's top level for a bird's-eye view of the Tower of London and the Thames, 43m (141 ft.) below. (Acrophobics need not apply.) ⏱ *1 hr. Tower Bridge.* ☎ *0207/403-3761. www. towerbridge.org.uk. £6 adults, £4.50 seniors, £3 kids 5–15. Ticket office is* on northwest side of bridge. Daily 9:30am–6pm. Tube: Tower Hill.

Tower Bridge, not London Bridge, is the most recognizable span in the city.

4 ★ kids **The Monument.** Sir Christopher Wren and Robert Hooke designed this 62m-high (203-ft.) Doric stone column—topped with a copper flame—to commemorate the Great Fire of 1666. That tragic disaster started on September 2 inside the house of a baker on Pudding Lane (the height of the tower corresponds to the distance from its base to the fire's starting point). A stiff wind ignited the old timber and thatch houses of medieval London; when the conflagration was finally stopped, more than 13,000 houses and 87 churches had been reduced to smoldering ashes. Closed for repairs in 2008, the tower's reopening in early 2009 should satisfy sightseers who are reluctant to climb its 311 steps with a new visitor center that will beam down live views from the top. ⏱ *50 min. Monument St.* ☎ *0207/ 626-2717. www.towerbridge.org.uk. Admission £5 adults, £3 seniors & kids. Daily 9:30am–5:30pm. Tube: Monument.*

5 ★★ kids **Tate Britain.** The Tate Britain, set on the former Thames-side site of the Millbank Penitentiary, opened in 1894 thanks to generous donations of money and art from sugar mogul Sir Henry Tate. One of England's most prestigious art

The Monument was built to commemorate the Great Fire of 1666.

Matisse's The Snail, *in the Tate Modern.*

museums, the Tate features a collection consisting chiefly of British art from the 16th century to the dawn of the 20th century. The museum has an unparalleled collection of works by renowned landscape artist J. M. W. Turner, who bequeathed most of his paintings to the museum. Other notable British artists whose works adorn the walls include satirist William Hogarth, illustrator William Blake, portraitist Thomas Gainsborough, and traditionalist Joshua Reynolds. ⏱ *2 hr. Millbank.* ☎ *0207/887-8008. www.tate.org.uk. Free admission, except for temporary exhibits. Daily 10am–6pm. Tube: Pimlico.*

The **6** ★★ **Tate Britain Restaurant** is one of the best museum eateries in London, and serves tasty modern British cuisine, accompanied by an extensive wine list, in a cheery, mural-filled dining room. It's a great place to stop for afternoon tea. *In the Tate Britain.* ☎ *0207/887-8825. $$.*

7 ★★★ kids **Tate Modern.** Britain's premier modern art museum, an offshoot of the Tate Britain, is housed in a gargantuan shell that was once a power station. For me, part of the fun of a visit here are the reminders of the building's utilitarian past—check out the

mmensity of the Turbine Hall and
wonder at the amount of electricity
nce provided to power the lights in
ondon. The museum's curators have
dmirably risen to the challenge of
lling its enormous space with
xhibits, gigantic sculptures, and art
nstallations. Collections here are dis-
layed thematically instead of by
eriod. Some of the world's most
mportant and exciting art is here,
with works by Dalí, Matisse, Picasso,
onnard, Duchamp, Giacometti, Man
ay, Bonnard, Diego Rivera, Mon-
rian, Klee, Margaret Bourke White,
rancis Bacon, David Hockney—
hink of the most groundbreaking
rtists of the past century and you
vill likely find something of their
work somewhere in this gargantuan
nd wonderfully satisfying cathedral
f modernity. Do use their brilliant
website to plan your visit if you can.
⏱ 2½ hr. Take a free guided theme
our or an audioguide highlights tour
€3) to make the best use of your

Warhol's Marilyn Diptych, *in the Tate
Modern.*

time. Bankside. ☎ *0207/887-8000.
www.tate.org.uk. Free admission
except for temporary exhibits. Daily
10am–6pm. Tube: Blackfriars.*

8 ★★★ kids **The British
Museum.** You could spend days
exploring this renowned museum. If
you're visiting on a Thursday or Friday, stay for the Late Night views
and enjoy the dark skies (no stars,
sadly) over the Great Court. ⏱ *1 hr.*
See p 30.

Sailing the Tate Boat

The Tate boat ferry service between the two Tate museums on
opposite banks of the Thames is one of London's better tourist cre-
ations. The same folks who built the London Eye designed the ferry's
dramatic Millbank Pier, and the colorful catamaran is itself a work of
art decorated by bad boy artist Damian Hirst. The 18-minute ride
runs from the Tate Britain to the Tate Modern, and also makes a stop
at the British Airways London Eye (p 12, **7**). When you're visiting
both Tate museums in a single day, the ferry is a convenient, scenic,
and comfortable way to get from one to the other.

Alas, it's not free. One-way ferry tickets cost £4
adults, £2 kids 5 to 15, free for kids 4 and under. If
you have a London Travelcard (p 159), you get a
good discount. Tickets can be bought online or
at the Tate Britain or Tate Modern. The boat
runs daily every 40 minutes (more often in high
season) between 10am and 6pm. For precise
boat times, call ☎ 0207/887-3959 or check
www.tate.org.uk/tatetotate.

The Tate Britain lit up at night.

The Best **in Three Days**

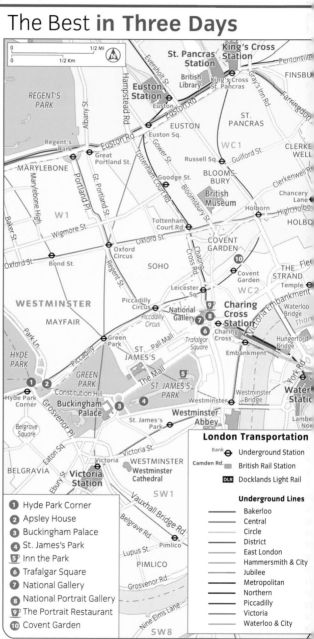

1. Hyde Park Corner
2. Apsley House
3. Buckingham Palace
4. St. James's Park
5. Inn the Park
6. Trafalgar Square
7. National Gallery
8. National Portrait Gallery
9. The Portrait Restaurant
10. Covent Garden

London Transportation

Bank ⊖ Underground Station

Camden Rd. ▇ British Rail Station

DLR Docklands Light Rail

Underground Lines

Bakerloo
Central
Circle
District
East London
Hammersmith & City
Jubilee
Metropolitan
Northern
Piccadilly
Victoria
Waterloo & City

This tour reveals London's great charms. I follow this route when I'm feeling out of sorts, and by the time I hit St. James's Park, I've fallen in love with London all over again. From the glory of Hyde Park Corner's monuments, to the incomparable art in the National Gallery, to the street crazies and entertainers of Covent Garden, this is the London that even crabby cabbies quietly relish as they go about their business. START: **Hyde Park Corner Tube Station**

1 ★ **Hyde Park Corner.** The busiest traffic circle in London is one of the city's most central locations, with Piccadilly, Knightsbridge, Park Lane, Constitution Hill, and Grosvenor Place radiating from its axis. It's the perfect place to get great morning photos of the majestic statue of *Winged Victory,* which replaced the statue of the Duke of Wellington in 1912 as a topper to the Wellington Arch. The arch itself was built in the 1820s to celebrate the British victory over the French. The underground walkways beneath the circle will save you from the treacherous crosswalks above and feature an interesting pictorial history of the Duke of Wellington, who orchestrated the crushing of Napoleon at Waterloo and remains one of Britain's most celebrated military heroes. ⏲ *10 min. Tube: Hyde Park Corner.*

2 ★★ **Apsley House.** Designed by famed architect Robert Adam, this neoclassical mansion was purchased by Arthur Wellesley, first Duke of Wellington (1769–1852), following his victories in the Napoleonic Wars. Its location, just past the old Knightsbridge tollgate, gave it the city's most grandiose address at the time: Number One London.

The dining room at Apsley House and its priceless Portuguese silver centerpiece.

The residence houses a renowned collection of decorative arts (many of the pieces bestowed upon the duke by grateful European monarchs), historic weaponry, numerous Old Masters, a towering nude statue of his enemy Napoleon (with a strategic fig leaf), and magnificent views of Hyde Park. It's a small, quick-hit museum that provides you with a taste of old Georgian splendor. (Don't miss the staggeringly over-the-top silver table setting, with an 8m-long/26-ft. centerpiece.) ⏲ *50 min. 149 Piccadilly.* ☎ *0207/499-5676. www. english-heritage.org.uk. Admission £5.30 adults, £4 seniors, £2.70 kids 5–15. Tues–Sun 10am–5pm. Tube: Hyde Park Corner.*

Wellington Arch, topped by the Winged Victory, sits atop Hyde Park Corner.

The Changing of the Guard at Buckingham Palace.

③ ★ Buckingham Palace. Buck House, the queen's famous abode in London (if the yellow-and-red Royal standard is flying, it means she's there), is the setting for the pageantry of the Changing of the Guard, a London tradition that attracts more people than it warrants—it's a nightmarish mass of crowds in the summer. A better place to see all the queen's horses and all the queen's men in action is the Horse Guards Parade (p 69, ③). But if you're determined to see the guards change here, arrive a half-hour early to get a seat by the statue of Victoria in front of the palace; it offers a reasonably good view. The ritual takes place every other day in winter and every day in summer at 11am in the forecourt of the palace. ⏱ 30 min. See p 45, ①.

④ ★★ kids St. James's Park. Arguably London's prettiest park, St. James's has an interesting history. The former swamp was tidied up in the 18th century, and evolved into a popular and notorious scene where prostitutes conducted business, laundresses brought their loads to dry on bushes, and drunken rakes took unsteady aim at dueling opponents. Now, however, it's very respectable, with a duck and pelican pond, weeping willows, and numerous paths lined with flower beds. The benches at the eastern end of the park offer a peaceful view of London's landmarks. ⏱ 30 min.

At the northeast end of St. James's Park is **⑤ ★★ kids Inn the Park,** a combination cafe and restaurant. Skip the expensive restaurant, where the food is overpriced; the same chefs supply the less-expensive cafeteria-style eatery, which features picturesque views of the London Eye and Whitehall. *In St James's Park (by Pall Mall).* ☎ 0207/451-9999. $.

⑥ Trafalgar Square. While you were once able to identify this famous square by its staggering population of pigeons, the practice of feeding them was outlawed (as were cars, to create a useful pedestrian area) in front of the National Gallery. The square is named after Britain's most revered naval hero, Horatio Viscount Nelson, who fell at the Battle of Trafalgar (the most pivotal naval battle of the Napoleonic Wars) in 1805, and whose statue stands on top of a 44m (144-ft.) pillar of granite guarded by kingly lions at the base. Street lamps at the Pall Mall end of the square are decorated with small replicas of the ships he commanded. The square is the scene of many rallies, demonstrations, and celebrations, and it's perfect for people-watching. ⏱ 15 min.

The statue of Horatio Viscount Nelson overlooking Trafalgar Square.

7 ★★★ kids **National Gallery.** his revered museum dominating rafalgar Square sits roughly where he stables of King Henry VIII used o be. Founded in 1832 with a collection of 38 paintings bought by the British government, the National is now home to some 2,000 works representing the world's major artistic periods from 1250 to 1900. It's London's best museum for anyone interested in the arts.

ational Gallery Highlights

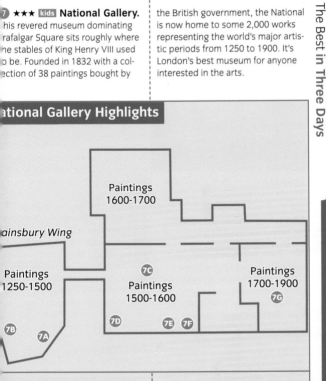

Start in the **7A** ★★★ **Sainsbury Wing's Room 56,** where you'll find familiar early European works, including Van Eyck's haunting portrait, *Arnolfini and His Wife.* Note the words inscribed over the mirror: JAN VAN EYCK WAS HERE/1434. For a contrast in mood, go to **7B** **Room 66** for Botticelli's *Venus & Mars,* a voluptuous allegory most likely painted as a backboard to decorate a bench or chest. The **7C** **West Wing's Room 10** holds Titian's *Bacchus & Ariadne* in colors still vibrant after 500 years; in **7D** **Room 8** is an ethereal Raphael painting of *The Madonna of the Pinks.* Holbein's

Ambassadors is in **7E** **Room 4;** the skull in the foreground was painted using a geometrical process called *anamorphosis,* distorting the image unless you look at it from an angle. Pay your respects to Michelangelo and da Vinci in **7F** **Room 2,** and then leave the Renaissance for the **7G** **East Wing** to see the works of Impressionists van Gogh, Monet, and Seurat, among others. ⏱ *2 hr. Trafalgar Sq. (at St. Martin's Lane).* ☎ *0207/747-2285. www.national gallery.org.uk. Free admission, except for temporary exhibits. Thurs–Tues 10am–6pm; Wed 10am–9pm. Tube: Leicester Sq.*

A portrait of William Shakespeare at the National Portrait Gallery.

⑧ ★★ kids **National Portrait Gallery.** Adjacent to the National Gallery, the NPG is the best place to put a face to the names of those who have shaped Britain politically, socially, and culturally. The gallery displays about 60% of its 10,000-plus portraits at a given time, ranging from King Harold II (b. 1022) to actress Keira Knightley (b. 1985). Familiar faces include Judi Dench, Richard Branson, Vivienne Westwood, Diana Rigg, David Bowie, Simon Cowell, Julie Christie, Michael Caine, and other less celebrated Brits, such as the psycho Kray brothers and their mum. Start at the top and work your way down. ⏱ *1 hr. 2 St. Martin's Lane, W1.* ☎ *0207/306-0055. www.npg.org.uk. Free admission, except for temporary exhibits. Sat–Wed 10am–6pm; Thurs–Fri 10am–9pm. Tube: Leicester Sq.*

🍴 ★★★ **The Portrait Restaurant,** on the top floor of the NPG, commands the most spectacular views over Trafalgar Square. The lounge area, serving salads, light meals, and afternoon tea, is your best bet for a quick bite. *National Portrait Gallery, 2 St. Martin's Lane, W1.* ☎ *0207/312-2490. $$.*

⑩ ★★★ kids **Covent Garden.** This famous marketplace—first laid out in the 17th century—is a good spot to end your day of cultural explorations. The area is bordered by the Strand, Charing Cross, Drury Lane, and High Holborn. At its heart is the Inigo Jones–designed arcade now filled with upscale shops and uninspired cafes. **Jubilee Market,** with inexpensive whatnots and cheap clothing, is set on the southern side of the arcade; at the western end you'll find stalls that, depending on the day, offer antiques, handmade crafts, or flea market goods. You may even be lucky enough to come upon an operatic performance given by professionals from the neoclassical **Royal Opera House** that faces the arcade. This area offers busking at its best; be it a tattooed man juggling knives, or a chamber music quartet, you'll always find real talent in Covent Garden's street entertainment. ⏱ *1–2 hr. Tube: Covent Garden.* ●

Colorful Covent Garden is a good spot for shopping and street entertainment.

The Best
Museum Tours

and let thy feet
millenniums hence
be set in midst of knowled

Victoria and Albert Museum

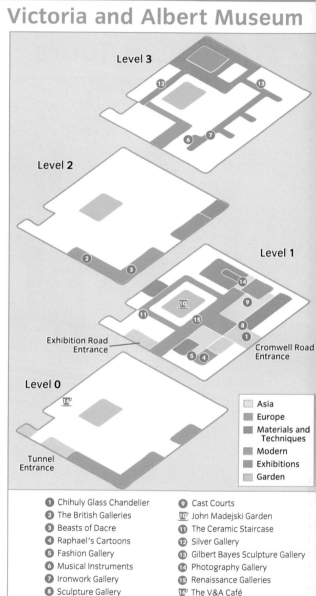

Level 3

Level 2

Level 1

Cromwell Road Entrance

Exhibition Road Entrance

Level 0

Tunnel Entrance

Asia
Europe
Materials and Techniques
Modern
Exhibitions
Garden

1 Chihuly Glass Chandelier
2 The British Galleries
3 Beasts of Dacre
4 Raphael's Cartoons
5 Fashion Gallery
6 Musical Instruments
7 Ironwork Gallery
8 Sculpture Gallery

9 Cast Courts
10 John Madejski Garden
11 The Ceramic Staircase
12 Silver Gallery
13 Gilbert Bayes Sculpture Gallery
14 Photography Gallery
15 Renaissance Galleries
16 The V&A Café

Previous page: The British Museum is home to one of the world's best collections of art and artifacts.

This museum's 13km (8 miles) of corridors are resplendent with the world's greatest collection of decorative arts. Opened in 1852 by Prince Albert, this treasure-trove, known as the V&A, is home to millions of pieces of priceless arts and crafts. A massive refurbishment continues to polish its glorious displays of paintings, furniture, glass, ceramics, silver, and fashion. START: **Tube to South Kensington**

1 ★★★ Chihuly Glass Chandelier. Renowned glass artist Dale Chihuly created this serpentine green and blue masterpiece specifically for the V&A in 2001, when an exhibition of his work was staged in the museum's outdoor courtyard. It's 8m (26 ft.) long, and made up of thousands of exquisite hand-blown glass baubles. Despite its airy effect, it weighs 3,800 pounds. *Foyer.* ⏱ 3 min.

2 ★★★ kids The British Galleries. This stellar example of 21st-century curatorship features some of England's greatest cultural treasures. The big draw is the **Great Bed of Ware** (Room 57), a masterpiece of woodcarving that earned mention in Shakespeare's *Twelfth Night*. Built in 1596 as a sales gimmick for an inn, the bed is now covered in I WAS HERE graffiti and wax seals left by centuries of visitors. Another highlight is the **Portrait of Margaret Laton** (Room 56); the painting is rather ordinary, but the jacket displayed alongside it is the very one worn in the portrait, which makes a stop here worthwhile. The interactive area will quell any kids' rebellions; my

The Great Bed of Ware is one of the V&A's top treasures.

favorite display allows you to design your own heraldic crest on a computer. ⏱ 1 hr.

3 ★★ Beasts of Dacre. These four carved heraldic animals (gryphon, bull, dolphin, and ram) were carved for the Dacres, one of northern England's most important families, in 1520. The wooden figures survived a fire in 1844, only to be restored in a rather gaudy, carousel-animal, Victorian style. Their weird whimsy has a wondrous dignity. *Stairway C.* ⏱ 5 min.

4 ★★★ Raphael's Cartoons. Dating back to 1521, these immense and expertly rendered drawings (*cartoon* is derived from the Italian word for a large piece of paper, *cartone*) were used by the artist Raphael to

A heraldic bull, one of the Beasts of Dacre.

plot a set of tapestries originally intended to hang in the Vatican's Sistine Chapel. *Room 48a.* ⏲ *15 min.*

5 ★★ **Fashion Gallery.** From a ludicrous 18th-century, 1.2m-wide (4-ft.) skirt to vertiginous platform shoes by Vivienne Westwood, this gallery is proof positive that every age has its share of fashion victims. *Room 40.* ⏲ *25 min.*

6 ★ **Musical Instruments.** This gallery displays a first-class collection of ivory and ebony inlaid guitars and lutes, as well as spinets, pianos, and virginals (including Elizabeth I's 1570 model—the Virgin Queen was reportedly quite the accomplished musician) that have been decorated to within an inch of their lives. *Room 40a.* ⏲ *20 min.*

7 ★★ **Ironwork Gallery.** Just past curlicued gates and a nostalgic display of cookie tins, you'll find this gallery's highlight—the stupendous **Hereford Screen,** a masterpiece of Victorian ironwork designed by the same man who devised the Albert Memorial (p 46, **5**). Check out the bird's-eye view of the foyer's chandelier. *Room 114.* ⏲ *20 min.*

8 ★★ **Sculpture Gallery.** Sarcophagi, marble founts, and alabaster busts of great beauty are just some of the treasures you'll find in this gallery. *Room 50a.* ⏲ *20 min.*

9 ★★★ **Cast Courts.** These two popular rooms used to be more colorfully titled "Fakes and Forgeries." Some of the counterfeit items are exceptional, executed with just as much skill as the originals. Among the imitations, you'll find a plaster cast of the statue of David (whose nudity so shocked Queen Victoria that she had a fig leaf made for it—it's now displayed behind the statue), a copy of Ghiberti's famous bronze doors for Florence's Baptistery, and an entire church facade. *Rooms 46a & 46b.* ⏲ *20 min.*

An 18th-century gown from the Fashion Gallery.

For a quick outdoor snack, grab a table or recline on the lush lawns of the **10** kids **John Madejski Garden**. The fountain is great fun for kids, and on a sunny day, you may not want to go back in the museum. The sandwiches and teatime treats are plentiful and well-priced. *Inner Courtyard. $.*

11 ★★ **The Ceramic Staircase.** The V&A's first director, Henry Cole, designed these stairs, intending to doll up all the museum's staircases in this ceramics-gone-mad style. For better or worse, when the costs for the staircase spiraled out of control in 1870, the project was quietly dropped. *Staircase I.* ⏲ *10 min.*

12 ★★ **Silver Gallery.** Possibly the museum's most impressive collection, this hall shimmers with a jaw-dropping array of over 10,000 silver objects, ranging from baby rattles to candelabras to bath-sized punch bowls. Highlights include the 19th-century, gem-encrusted Burgess Cup; a rare, engraved 17th-century silver flask that belonged to the illegitimate son of Charles II and his mistress, actress Nell Gwynn; and a modern blouse made of silver mesh. Check out the interactive educational displays to learn some secrets of silver smithery. **Rooms 65–70a.** 🕐 25 min.

The ornate Burgess Cup is just one of the V&A's silver treasures.

⑬ ★★ **Gilbert Bayes Sculpture Gallery.** This collection of small European sculpture in every imaginable medium is (currently) in an enviable position: It's off the elegant but dimly lit Leighton Hall (check out the floor tiles) and gives you a treetop view of the Cast Courts, allowing you to inspect the dramatic details on the top of the stone church facade below. **Room 111.** 🕐 20 min.

⑭ ★★★ **Photography Gallery.** The V&A's vast and outstanding collection of images (some 300,000) was started in 1852. Works from as far back as 1839 are shown on a rotating basis. You might see prints by noted British shutterbugs Julia Cameron and Bill Brandt, or early daguerreotypes. **Room 38a.** 🕐 15 min.

⑮ ★★★ **Renaissance Galleries.** A mélange of mediums from the creatively fertile Renaissance era (1200–1650) is on display here, including tapestries, stained glass, statuary, glass, and metalwork. Notable items include a 15th-century Murano glass goblet and a 15th-century stained-glass panel of Holy Roman Emperor Maximilian I that originally hung in Bruges's Chapel of the Holy Blood. **Rooms 21–25.** 🕐 30 min.

Stop at the newly designed ⑯ **V&A Café** to admire this splendid cafeteria, overlooked by Arts and Crafts stained glass and ornate ceramics and tiles. The food includes traditional hot English fare, plus sandwiches and salads—delicious dining at cafeteria prices. **Ground Level. $.**

The V&A: Practical Matters

The Victoria and Albert Museum (☎ 0207/942-2000; www.vam.ac.uk) is located at Cromwell Road, SW7, off Exhibition Road. Take the Tube to South Kensington and follow the signs to the museum.

Admission is free, except to special exhibits. The museum is open daily from 10am to 5:45pm. On Friday, the V&A stays open until 10pm for the Late View, when live music, guided tours, and lectures are offered (it's best for adults). On weekends and school holidays, there are special activities for kids of all ages.

The British Museum

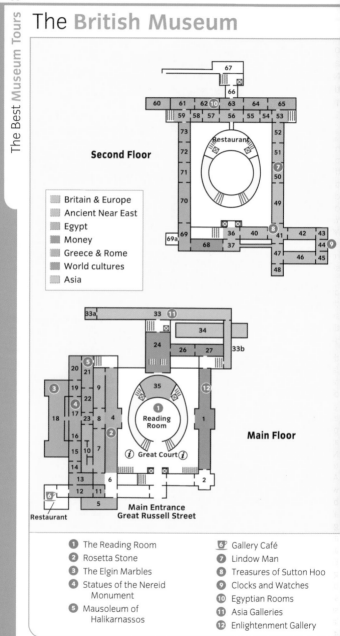

Second Floor

- Britain & Europe
- Ancient Near East
- Egypt
- Money
- Greece & Rome
- World cultures
- Asia

Main Floor

Reading Room

Great Court

Main Entrance
Great Russell Street

Restaurant

1 The Reading Room
2 Rosetta Stone
3 The Elgin Marbles
4 Statues of the Nereid Monument
5 Mausoleum of Halikarnassos
6 Gallery Café
7 Lindow Man
8 Treasures of Sutton Hoo
9 Clocks and Watches
10 Egyptian Rooms
11 Asia Galleries
12 Enlightenment Gallery

The British Museum, started with a donation by collector Sir Hans Sloane in 1753, opened at a time when the expansion of the British Empire into just about every corner of the earth ensured that its collection would be as eclectic as it was priceless. Note the frieze above the entrance—it signifies the museum's intention to encompass all the branches of science and art. START: **Holborn Tube Station**

❶ ★★ **The Reading Room.** This hallowed place of literary history has been restored to its 1857 grandeur. If the circular stacks of books and the crowning gilt-and-azure dome don't get you, turn around and look on either side of the entrance doors. You'll find a list of authors (Dickens, Marx, Tennyson, Kipling, and Darwin, among others) who sat in this very room to write, think, and research some of literature's finest works. There's a children's section, but quiet must be observed. A free multimedia database here allows you to search the museum's vast collections. 🕑 *15 min.*

❷ ★★★ **Rosetta Stone.** One of the museum's most highly prized artifacts is an ancient text engraved on a tablet in three scripts (hieroglyphic, demotic, and Greek) and two languages (Greek and Egyptian) that enumerates the virtues of 13-year-old pharaoh Ptolemy V, who lived in 196 B.C. The tablet was found in 1799 by Napoleon's troops and handed over to the British Army as part of the Alexandria Treaty of 1802. The text was deciphered in 1822, a breakthrough that allowed archaeologists and historians to decode ancient Middle Eastern hieroglyphics, and proved that these symbols represented a spoken language. *Room 4.* 🕑 *5 min.*

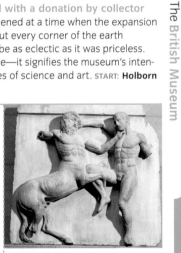

A frieze from the Parthenon, one of the famous Elgin Marbles.

❸ ★★★ **The Elgin Marbles.** The Greek government has been fighting for 2 centuries to get these detailed classical sculptures and artifacts—taken from the Parthenon by Lord Elgin in 1805—returned to Athens. The B.M. argues that it has provided a safe home for these carvings (including 75m/246 ft. of the original temple frieze), which would otherwise have been chipped away by vandals or degraded by remaining in the open air. The marbles may yet be returned to the Parthenon (a disastrous precedent for the museum, filled as it is with the booty of the world), but don't expect them to depart the B.M. anytime soon. *Room 18.* 🕑 *20 min.*

❹ ★ **Statues of the Nereid Monument.** This 4th-century-B.C. Lykian tomb from southwest

The Rosetta Stone, one of the most significant artifacts in the world.

Turkey arrived at the museum with the Elgin Marbles in 1816, and its lifelike statuary is almost surreal. Even without their heads, the daughters of the sea god Nereus (aka Nereids) look as graceful as the ocean waves they are meant to personify. *Room 17.* ⏱ *5 min.*

An early Anglo-Saxon helmet that's one of the Treasures of Sutton Hoo.

5 ★★ **Mausoleum of Halikarnassos.** These are the remains of one of the Seven Wonders of the Ancient World—the breathtaking Ionian Greek tomb built for King Maussollos, from whose name the word "mausoleum" is derived. The tomb remained undisturbed from 351 B.C. to medieval times, when an earthquake damaged it. In 1494, Crusaders used its stones to fortify a castle refuge; in 1846, sections of the tomb's frieze were found at the castle and given to the B.M. Subsequent excavations turned up the remarkably lifelike horse sculpture and the series of lounging figures. *Room 21.* ⏱ *15 min.*

The excellent **6** ★★ kids **Gallery Café** is a relaxed, cafeteria-style eatery decorated with the 1801 casts of the Elgin Marbles. The hot meals, sandwiches, and desserts are all reasonably priced. *Off Room 12.* ☎ *0207/323-8990. $.*

7 Lindow Man. Don't miss the affecting cadaver of the "Bog Man" (aka "Pete Marsh"), preserved in a peat bog in Lindow Moss, Cheshire, for nearly 2,000 years (he was found in 1984). The poor man was struck on the head, garroted, knifed, and then put head first into the bog! The excessiveness of his premortem wounds suggests he died in a Druidic sacrificial ritual. *End of Room 50, on your right.* ⏱ *5 min.*

8 ★★★ **Treasures of Sutton Hoo.** Sutton Hoo was a burial ground of the early Anglo-Saxons (including one royal, who literally went down with his 30m/98-ft. oak ship). When this tomb was excavated in 1939, previous beliefs about the inferior arts and crafts of England's Dark Age (ca. A.D. 625) were confounded, as well-designed musical instruments, glassware, armor, and even Byzantine articles (don't miss the exquisitely detailed Wilton Cross) were uncovered. *Room 41.* ⏱ *15 min.*

9 ★★ **Clocks and Watches.** The museum's outstanding collection of timepieces features the mind-blowing Galleon (or "Nef") Clock, which used to roll along a table announcing dinnertime to guests. Built (in 1865 in Germany) to resemble a medieval galleon, the gilt-copper marvel played music, beat drums, and even fired tiny cannons for emphasis. *Room 39.* ⏱ *20 min.*

10 ★★★ **Egyptian Rooms.** It's said that the ghost of one of the 3,000-year-old mummies on display roams these rooms. Room 62 has a **mummified cat,** while Room 63 is filled with coffins, funerary objects, and a papyrus page from **The Book of the Dead** illustrating the necessary steps to a peaceful afterlife. In Room 64 you will usually find the 5,000-year-old carcass of a man the museum calls **"Ginger,"** whose body dried out naturally in the desert. (His preserved red hair earned him the nickname.) ⏱ *30 min.*

Practical Matters

The British Museum (☎ 0207/636-1555; www.thebritishmuseum.ac.uk) is located on Great Russell Street. Take the Tube to the Tottenham Court Road, Russell Square, or Holborn station.

Admission is free, except to temporary special exhibits. The museum is open daily from 10am to 5:30pm; on Thursday and Friday, select galleries remain open until 8:30pm. A variety of specialty tours of the museum are offered, ranging from self-guided audio tours for families to free, 50-minute introductory tours; check the website for details or inquire at the Information Desk in the museum's Great Court. The website's "Compass" database offers access to data on thousands of the museum's objects.

The bronze figure of Nataraja (Dancing Shiva) in the Asian Galleries.

⓫ ★★ **Asia Galleries.** Room 33 is an oasis of calm that lures you with the serenity of meditating Buddhas and the grace of the *Dancing Shiva*—a bronze sculpture depicting one of India's most famous images. The intricate frieze of the **Great Stupa** (Room 33a) carved in India in the 3rd century B.C. so closely resembles the Elgin Marbles that you'll wonder about the artistic zeitgeist that seems to pass unaided through borders and cultures. There are statues of bodhisattvas, Buddhist archetypes, in every medium—from porcelain to metal. As you exit through Room 33b, be sure to look at the **Chinese jade carvings** (some are over 4,000 years old). ⏰ 20 min.

The coffin of Cleopatra.

⓬ **Enlightenment Gallery.** "Discovering the World in the 18th Century" is the subtitle of this permanent exhibit, located in the restored King's Library. Designed for George III by Sir Robert Smirke, the room is regarded as the finest and largest neoclassical interior hall in London. You'll be reaching for your pince-nez and quill pen as you marvel at the polished mahogany bookshelves stuffed with rare books, and eagerly examine the display cases filled with some 5,000 items that demonstrate the far-reaching, eclectic passions of the 18th-century Enlightenment scholar—the exact kind of person who made the British Museum possible. ⏰ 30 min.

London's Best Small Museums

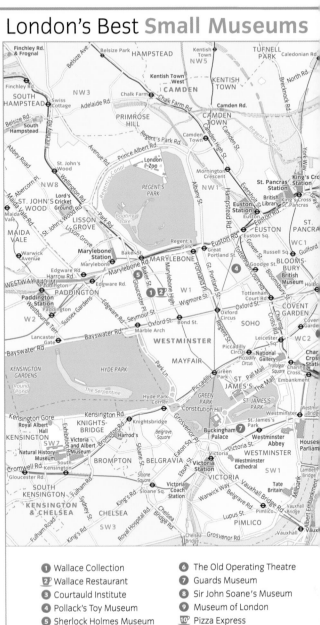

1. Wallace Collection
2. Wallace Restaurant
3. Courtauld Institute
4. Pollack's Toy Museum
5. Sherlock Holmes Museum
6. The Old Operating Theatre
7. Guards Museum
8. Sir John Soane's Museum
9. Museum of London
10. Pizza Express

London Transportation

Bank ⊖	Underground Station
Camden Rd. ▬	British Rail Station
DLR	Docklands Light Rail

Underground Lines

Bakerloo
Central
Circle
District
East London
Hammersmith & City
Jubilee
Metropolitan
Northern
Piccadilly
Victoria
Waterloo & City

If you suffer from sore feet and info-overload when visiting huge museums or you dislike milling crowds, you'll be delighted by the charms of London's many smaller museums. These are often housed in beautiful old mansions whose appealing architectural details can be as fascinating as the items on view. Most of these lesser-known gems aren't mobbed by visitors, so you can take your time when inspecting the unique collections, which may reflect the taste of their original owners (Sir John Soane's Museum) or reveal the artistic leanings of an entire age (the Wallace Collection).

START: **Bond St. Tube Station**

1 ★★★ Wallace Collection.

This collection offers an astonishing glimpse into the buying power of the English gentry after the French Revolution, when important art and furnishings were made homeless by the guillotine. In the late 19th century, this entire mansion and its contents were left to the nation by Lady Wallace on the condition that they be kept intact, without additions or subtractions. The paintings are breathtaking, with works by Titian, Gainsborough, Rembrandt, Hals (including his famous *Laughing Cavalier*), and others. But the most fascinating aspect of the collection is the rare opportunity to view exceptional art in a house whose architectural details, fine furniture, and Sèvres tableware give visitors a glimpse into a vanished aristocratic world. ⏲ *1 hr. Arrive at opening. Hertford House, Manchester Sq.* ☎ *0207/563-9500. www.wallace collection.org. Free admission. Open daily 10am–5pm. Tube: Bond St.*

Pause at the Wallace Collection's French brasserie–style 2 ★★ **Wallace Restaurant,** which serves up well-prepared meals inside a pleasant glass-covered and sculpture-filled atrium. It's a lovely place to rest your legs while indulging in a cup of tea. ☎ *0207/563-9500. $$.*

3 ★★★ Courtauld Institute.

Housed inside Somerset House, a Georgian romp of a château whose centerpiece is a public courtyard (with an ice rink in winter and a picturesque fountain in summer), the

One of the Wallace Collection's ornately furnished rooms.

Van Gogh's Self-Portrait with Bandaged Ear, in the Courtauld Institute.

St. www.pollockstoymuseum.com. Admission £4 adults, £3 seniors, £2 children. Daily 10am–5pm. Tube: Tottenham Court Rd.

⑤ ★★ kids The Sherlock Holmes Museum. Even for those not particularly *au fait* with the fictional detective, this is a weird and wonderful museum that captures a time and place in 19th-century London better than many historical sites. Holmes fans will be entertained by the many clever details of Sherlock's obsessions and pastimes scattered throughout the house. ⏱ *45 min. 221b Baker St.* ☎ *0207/935-8866. www.sherlock-holmes.co.uk. Admission £6 adults, £4 children ages 6–15, free to kids 5 & under. Daily 9:30am–6pm. Tube: Baker St.*

⑥ ★★★ kids The Old Operating Theatre. A visit here will cure any complaints about modern medicine. The wooden operating table with leather restraints used for performing surgery; an early pair of forceps, and other instruments of outdated medical practices will give you a good dose of the willies. ⏱ *30 min. 9a St. Thomas's St.*

Courtauld is a choice destination for art lovers. The institute is especially celebrated for its Impressionist collection (van Gogh and Manet among others), but it is also home to works by such masters as Botticelli, Rubens, and Brueghel. ⏱ *30 min.* ☎ *0207/ 848-2526. www. somerset-house. org.uk. Museum admission free Mon 10am–2pm. Admission other days £5 adults, £4 seniors, free to kids 17 & under. Daily 10am–6pm. Tube: Charing Cross.*

Step right into the world of Sir Arthur Conan Doyle's famous detective at the Sherlock Holmes Museum.

☎ *0207/955-4791. www.thegarret. org.uk. Admission £5.45 adults, £4.45 seniors, £3 to kids 15 & under. Daily 10:30am–5pm. Tube: London Bridge.*

④ ★★★ Pollock's Toy Museum. Since its inception in 1852, Pollack's has delighted children of all ages with its old puppet theater, tin windup toys, and priceless dolls from around the world. The toy shop on the ground floor of this rickety old building is a lot of fun. ⏱ *40 min.* ☎ *0207/636-3452. 1 Scala*

⑦ ★★ kids Guards Museum. If you've wondered about the many extravagant get-ups worn by the five regiments of the Queen's Guards, or longed to try on one of the huge bearskin hats they wear, drop in here and learn about it all.

The former home of Sir John Soane now displays the noted architect's collection of antiques and paintings.

🕐 *30 min. Wellington Barracks, Birdcage Walk.* ☎ *0207/955-4791. www.theguardsmuseum.com. Admission £3 adults, free to kids 15 & under. Daily 10am–4pm. Tube: St. James.*

8 ★★ **Sir John Soane's Museum.** The distinguished British architect Sir John Soane (1753–1837) was also an avid collector. His former home in Lincoln Fields is a testament to his skill as an architect (the use of interior space enabled an immense number of antiquities and paintings to be stuffed into the house) and to the breadth of his hobby. The bulk of the collection was amassed between the late 18th and early 19th centuries, when antiquities could be removed from their country of origin and displayed casually in one's home. Ancient tablets, sculptures, paintings (including William Hogarth's celebrated *Rake's Progress*), architectural models, and even an Egyptian sarcophagus are strewn around in no particular order,

and the haphazardness of the display is part of the museum's charm. 🕐 *1 hr. 13 Lincoln Inn Fields.* ☎ *0207/405-2107. www.soane.org. Free admission. Tues–Sat 10am–5pm. Tube: Holborn.*

9 ★★★ kids **Museum of London.** If it has to do with London's history, you'll find it at this incredibly comprehensive museum. Reconstructions of 19th-century shops and Anderson bomb shelters from World War II are just two of the time-travel displays at this wonderful location. The exhibits start at the prehistoric level and proceed to the 21st century, with stops at all the great and terrible moments of London's long life. Do not miss the ornate Lord Mayor's Coach, a 3-ton gilt affair in which Cinderella would have felt right at home. 🕐 *1½ hr. London Wall.* ☎ *0207/600-3699. www.museumoflondon.org.uk. Free admission, except for temporary exhibits. Mon–Sat 10am–6pm; Sun noon–5:50pm. Tube: St. Paul's.*

Conveniently located next to the Museum of London is **10** **Pizza Express,** a branch of one of London's better pizza chains. You'll also find generous servings of well-priced salads, pastas, and delicious desserts. Service is very efficient. *125 Alban Gate, London Wall.* ☎ *0207/600-8880. $$.* ●

The fairy-tale Lord Mayor's Coach is the star attraction at the Museum of London.

The Best Special-Interest Tours

Kids' London

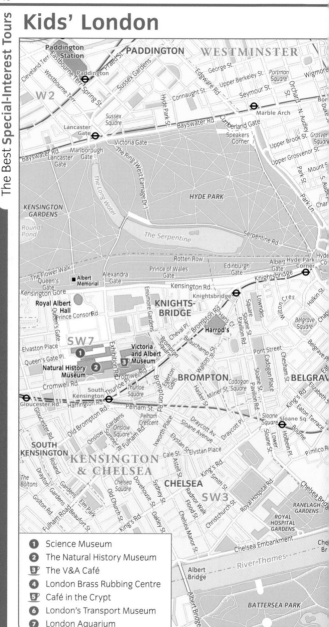

1. Science Museum
2. The Natural History Museum
3. The V&A Café
4. London Brass Rubbing Centre
5. Café in the Crypt
6. London's Transport Museum
7. London Aquarium

Previous page: The gilded gates that guard the entrance to Kensington Palace.

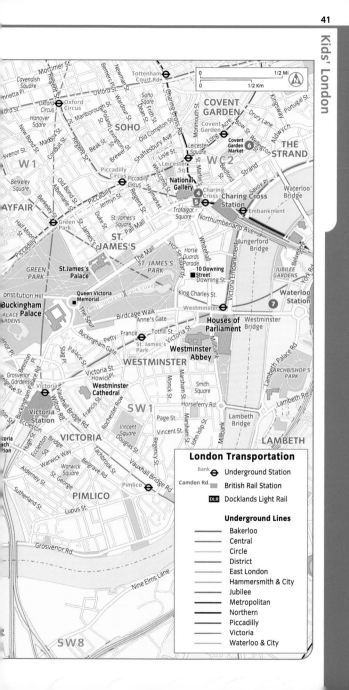

0   1/2 Mi
0   1/2 Km

COVENT
GARDEN

Tottenham
Court Rd.

Cavendish
Square

Mortimer St.

Regent St.

Berners St.

Newman St.

Charing Cross Rd.

Wardour St.

Poland St.

Gt. Marlborough St.

Kingsway

Drury Lane

Portugal St.

henrietta Pl.

Oxford   Oxford
Circus   Circus

Oxford St.

Hanover
Sqare

Soho
Square

Frith St.

Dean St.

Old Compton St.

Covent
Garden

Long Acre

Bow St.

Wellington St.

Aldwych

THE
STRAND

Ford St.

New Bond St.

Maddox St.

Conduit St.

Old Bond St.

Albemarle St.

Beak St.

Brewer St.

Lexington St.

Shaftesbury Ave.

Wardour St.

Old Compton St.

Monmouth St.

Leicester
Square

Covent
Garden
Market   6

St. Martin's La.

Bedford St.

Strand

Savoy Pl.

WC2

svenor St.

Regent St.

Berkeley
Square

Piccadilly
Circus   Piccadilly
         Circus

Jermyn St.

Haymarket

Lisle St.

Leicester
Sq.

National
Gallery   4

Charing
Cross

5

Charing Cross
Station

Embankment

Waterloo
Bridge

W 1

AYFAIR

Berkeley St.

Albemarle St.

PICCADILLY

Duke St.

St. James's
Square

Pall Mall

Trafalgar
Square

Northumberland Ave.

Hungerford
Bridge

Waterloo Bridge

Belvedere Rd.

Hall Moon St.

Piccadilly

Green Park

St. James's St.

The Mall

ST.
JAMES'S

Horse Guards Rd.

Horse
Guards
Parade

Whitehall

Victoria Embankment

JUBILEE
GARDENS

York Rd.

GREEN
PARK

St. James's
Palace

ST. JAMES'S
PARK

10 Downing
Street
Downing St.

Waterloo
Station

7

onstitution Hill

Queen Victoria
Memorial

St. James's Park Lake

Birdcage Walk

Anne's Gate

King Charles St.

Westminster

Buckingham
ALACE   Palace
ARDENS

The Spur

Buckingham Gate

Petty France

Tothill St.

St. James's
Park

Victoria St.

Houses of
Parliament

Westminster
Bridge

Westminster

enor Pl.

Palace St.

Stag Pl.

Westminster
Abbey

WESTMINSTER

Millbank

Lambeth Palace Rd.

ARCHBISHOP'S
PARK

Grosvenor
Gardens
elgrave St.

Beeston Pl.

Buckingham Palace Rd.

Victoria St.

Howick Pl.

Westminster
Cathedral

Monck St.

Marsham St.

Smith
Square

Lambeth Rd.

Victoria
Station

Wilton Rd.

Francis St.

SW1

ton St.

Eccleston

Hugh St.

Eccleston Bridge

Rochester Row

Vincent
Square

Page St.

Vincent St.

Regency St.

John Islip St.

Millbank

Lambeth
Bridge

ictoria
ach
tion

Warwick Way

Tachbrook St.

Douglas St.

Vauxhall Bridge Rd.

LAMBETH

Alderney St.

Warwick
Square

St. George

Belgrave Rd.

Pimlico

PIMLICO

Lupus St.

Sutherland St.

Grosvenor Rd.

Nine Elms Lane

SW8

London Transportation

Bank ⊖ Underground Station

Camden Rd. ▪ British Rail Station

DLR Docklands Light Rail

Underground Lines

——— Bakerloo
——— Central
——— Circle
——— District
——— East London
——— Hammersmith & City
——— Jubilee
——— Metropolitan
——— Northern
——— Piccadilly
——— Victoria
——— Waterloo & City

The Best Special-Interest Tours

L ondon is one of Europe's best playgrounds for kids. Nearly all the city's major museums have developed well-thought-out activities to entertain and inspire kids on weekends and show off the collections to their best advantage. Whether you make it to all the venues on this tour obviously depends on the temperaments and ages of your children. START: **South Kensington Tube Station**

One of the many interactive exhibits at the Science Museum.

1 ★★★ kids **Science Museum.** Designed to appeal to children of all ages, this great institution offers consistently arresting exhibits with fun features, including The Garden, an interactive play area for 3- to 6-year-olds on the Lower Ground Floor. Its seven levels of displays succeed in getting both kids and adults to understand the place of science in everyday life, even as they provide hours of amusement. Highlights include "Launchpad" (hands-on chemistry and physics fun), Foucault's Pendulum, the Apollo 10 command module, and

an IMAX theater (which charges a fee—buy your tickets as soon as you arrive). The gift shop is almost as interesting as the exhibits. ⏱ *2 hr. Come weekdays to avoid weekend throngs. Exhibition Rd.* ☎ *0870/870-4868. www.sciencemuseum.org.uk. Free admission, except for special exhibits. Daily 10am–6pm. Tube: S. Kensington.*

2 ★★★ kids **The Natural History Museum.** This museum's building alone is worth a look. Statues of beasts have been incorporated into its facade; and in the lobby, you'll find charming stained-glass windows. Although not as edgy and modern as the Science Museum next door, this museum is no fossil. Its exhibits include modern dinosaur displays and an interactive rainforest. The gem, mineral, and meteorite exhibits are all top-notch. The old animal dioramas are still around, but the new Darwin Wing (a £70-million project years in the making) has left them in the dust; its highlights include ongoing events with naturalists, photographers, and explorers (not to mention its 28 million insects and 6 million plant specimens). ⏱ *1½ hr. Cromwell Rd., off Exhibition Rd.* ☎ *0207/942-5000. www.nhm.ac.uk. Free admission,*

One of many animal carvings on the facade of the Natural History Museum.

except for temporary exhibits. *Daily 10am–6pm. Tube: S. Kensington.*

3 kids **The V&A Café** has been relocated and expanded around the museum's original tea venues, the Morris, Gamble, and Poynter Rooms (p 29). It's a pleasant venue where families can enjoy a wide selection of hot meals (roasts and vegetarian options), deli sandwiches, delicious desserts, and great teatime treats. *Victoria & Albert Museum, Cromwell Rd.* ☎ *0207/942-2000. $.*

4 ★★★ kids **London Brass Rubbing Centre.** Inside the crypt of St. Martin-in-the-Fields are 88 bronze plates of medieval subjects that kids (and adults) can reproduce by rubbing a waxy crayon over a piece of paper affixed to the plate. Admission is free, but rubbings start at £4.50 for a small drawing (a life-size knight will set you back £20). Kids love how they can produce impressive works of art with just a little effort. The Centre also sells great souvenirs. ⏱ *1 hr. St. Martin-in-the-Fields, Trafalgar Sq.* ☎ *0207/766-1122. Free admission; rubbings from £4.50. Mon–Wed 10am–6pm; Thurs–Sat 10am–9pm; Sun noon–6pm.*

Also in the basement of St. Martin-in-the-Fields Church, **5** ★ **Café in the Crypt** is a handy, no-fuss cafe that serves hot lunches, snacks, sweets, and drinks. *St. Martin-in-the-Fields, Trafalgar Sq.* ☎ *0207/839-4342. Tube: Charing Cross. $.*

6 ★★★ kids **London's Transport Museum.** If only the real London Transport system were as up-to-date and well-maintained as this museum. Climb aboard a stage-coach, a double-decker omnibus, or an early underground train. The new

London's Transport Museum features lots of family-friendly hands-on exhibits.

exhibits haven't neglected other modes of transport in this huge city: Bicycles, motorcycles, and taxis all get their close-ups at this fascinating museum. There's plenty of interactive fun as you trace the evolution of London's public transport through photos, films, old vehicles, and more. ⏱ *1½ hr. Covent Garden Piazza.* ☎ *0207/379-6344. www.ltmuseum. co.uk. Admission £10 adults, £8 seniors, £6.50 students, free for kids 15 & under. Sat–Thurs 10am–6pm; Fri 11am–9pm. Tube: Covent Garden.*

7 ★★ kids **London Aquarium.** You'd expect a bit more for your money at one of Europe's top aquariums, but when it comes down to it, kids adore this place. There's a pet-ting tank of manta rays, a simulated coral reef with sea horses, and appropriately scary shark tanks. ⏱ *1 hr. County Hall, Westminster Bridge Rd.* ☎ *0207/967-8000. www. londonaquarium.co.uk. Admission £13 adults; £11 seniors, students & kids 15–17 (bring ID); £9.75 kids 3–14; free for kids 2 & under; £44 family. 25% discount for purchasing tickets online. Daily 10am–6pm. Tube: Westminster.*

Kids love making brass rubbings at St. Martin-in-the-Fields.

Royal London

1 Buckingham Palace
2 Queen's Gallery
3 Palace Lounge
4 Royal Mews
5 Albert Memorial
6 Kensington Palace

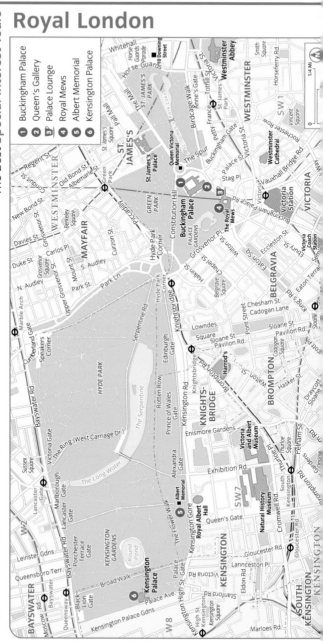

The various justifications for keeping the institution of the English monarchy inevitably come down to the entertainment of tourists, who can't get enough of the wealth, history, and gossip that have always defined royalty. This full-day tour serves up some of the city's royal highlights and offers a glimpse into the London lives of royals past and present. START: **Green Park Tube Station**

A gilded royal insignia on the gates of Buckingham Palace.

1 ★★ Buckingham Palace. The main draw of Queen Elizabeth II's official residence—a magnificent 500-room house that Queen Victoria despaired of ever making livable—is its exclusivity: It's open only in August and September, when the queen is not at home. The palace was originally built for the Duke of Buckingham and sold to King George III (who needed the room for his 15 kids) in 1761. George IV had it remodeled by famed architect John Nash in the 1820s, and the grandiose State Rooms you tour today remain virtually unchanged from his time. As an attraction, the treasure-laden palace has an

aloofness that may cause you to question its cost and effort, but it can't be beat for a look at one of the gilded cages of English royalty. ⏱ *2 hr. Book the earliest timed tour possible via the website to avoid the worst of the lines. Buckingham Palace Rd. ☎ 0207/766-7300. www. royalcollection.org.uk. Admission (includes self-guided audio tour) £16 adults, £14 over 60, £8.75 kids 5–16, £40 family. Aug–Sept daily 9:45am–3.45pm. Tube: Green Park.*

2 ★★ Queen's Gallery. This well-curated museum answers the question of how one furnishes and decorates a palace or two. Priceless treasures from the queen's private collection of paintings, jewelry, furniture, and bibelots are displayed in sumptuous Georgian-style surroundings. The exhibits rotate (the queen's holdings include, among other items, 10,000 Old Masters and enough objets d'art to fill several palaces—which they do when they aren't here), but whatever is on display will be top-notch. A highlight on my last visit to the gallery was an 18th-century silver vanity table—imagine having to polish that. You'll also find the city's best gift shop for royalty-related items, both cheap and dear. ⏱ *1½ hr. Buckingham Gate. ☎ 0207/766-7301.*

One of the many priceless treasures on display at the Queen's Gallery.

www.royalcollection.org.uk. Timed tickets necessary in summer. Admission £8.50 adults, £7.50 seniors, £4.25 kids 5–16, free for kids 4 & under. Daily 10am–4:30pm. Tube: Green Park.

Overlooking the entrance to the Royal Mews is the **3** **Palace Lounge,** an atmospheric spot to grab a cup of tea or a tasty light meal. Lucky visitors may get a glimpse of deliveries being made to Buckingham Palace in old-fashioned wagons. *In the Rubens at the Palace, 39 Buckingham Palace Rd. ☎ 0207/ 834-6600. $$.*

4 ★ **kids** **Royal Mews.** This oddly affecting royal experience is a great diversion on its own, or if you're waiting for your timed entry to Buckingham Palace. Even if you're not into horses, you'll be fascinated by this peek into the lives of the queen's privileged equines. The stalls at this working stable are roomy, the tack is pristine, and the ceremonial carriages (including the ornate Gold State Coach and the coach Princess Diana rode to her wedding to Prince Charles) are eye-popping. A small exhibit tells you about the role the queen's horses have played in the past and present; old sepia-toned pictures show various royals and

You can visit the queen's horses and carriages at the Royal Mews.

The Albert Memorial, Queen Victoria's elaborate shrine to her husband.

their four-footed friends. 🕑 *45 min. Buckingham Gate. ☎ 0207/766-7302. www.royalcollection.org.uk. Admission £7.50 adults, £6.75 seniors, £4.80 kids 5–16. March–July and Oct Sat–Thurs 11am–4pm; Aug–Sept Daily 10am–5pm (closed Nov–Feb). Tube: Green Park.*

5 ★ **kids** **Albert Memorial.** An inconsolable Queen Victoria spent an obscene amount of public money on this 55m-tall (180-ft.) shrine to her husband Albert, who died of typhoid fever in 1861. The project (completed in 1876) didn't go down too well with many of her ministers, but Victoria was not a woman to whom one said no. The excessively ornate mass of gilt, marble, statuary, and mosaics set in Kensington Gardens was restored (to the tune of millions of pounds) in the 1990s, and now stands in all its dubious glory across the street from the equally fabulous (and somewhat more useful) Albert Hall. That book Albert is holding is a catalogue from the Great Exhibition of which he was patron, and which formed the basis for the great museums of South Kensington (which was once called Albertropolis). 🕑 *30 min. Kensington Gardens (west of Exhibition Rd.). Free admission. Daily dawn–dusk. Tube: Kensington High St.*

6 ★★ kids Kensington Palace.
Once the 17th-century country refuge of monarchs William III and Mary II, this former home of Princess Diana is more satisfying to visit than Buckingham Palace (and it's open year-round). The palace is smaller, has more personality, and is more manageable to tour than Buckingham, with a number of pleasing architectural details that span the years from Jacobean England to the early 19th century.

Kensington Palace Highlights

William III's Small Bedchamber is now called the **6A ★★ 18th-Century Dress Rooms,** housing samples of the flamboyant clothing worn by the ladies and gentlemen of the royal court from 1750 to 1770. They're also home to the Royal Ceremonial Dress Collection, which features gowns worn by the queen and the late Princess Diana. The **6B ★ King's Grand Staircase** has a magnificent wrought-iron balustrade; its elaborate 16th-century-style Italianate murals on the walls and ceiling were commissioned by George I in 1725. The lavishly decorated **6C ★★ Cupola Room** features elaborately carved chandeliers, a breathtaking gilt clock, and a magnificent painted ceiling.

6D ★ Queen Victoria's Bedroom, hung with artwork commissioned by Victoria and Albert, is where the young princess and her mother slept until the teenager ascended the throne in 1837. **6E ★ Queen Mary's Bedchamber** was likely the room where Mary II died of smallpox in 1694; the bed, however, probably belonged to James II.
🕐 *2 hr. The Broad Walk, Kensington Gardens.* ☎ *0844/482-7777. www.hrp.org.uk. Admission (includes self-guided audio tour) £12 adults, £11 seniors, £6.15 kids 5–15, free for kids 4 & under. Daily 10am–5pm. Tube: Kensington High St.*

A gown worn by the late Princess Diana on display in Kensington Palace.

Hampton Court Palace

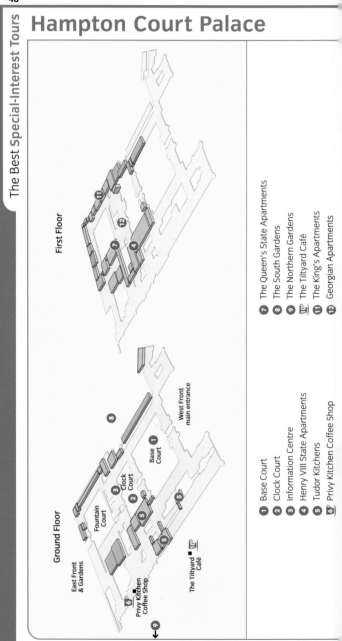

First Floor

Ground Floor

East Front & Gardens

Privy Kitchen Coffee Shop

Fountain Court

Clock Court

Base Court

West Front main entrance

The Tiltyard Café

1 Base Court
2 Clock Court
3 Information Centre
4 Henry VIII State Apartments
5 Tudor Kitchens
6 Privy Kitchen Coffee Shop

7 The Queen's State Apartments
8 The South Gardens
9 The Northern Gardens
10 The Tiltyard Café
11 The King's Apartments
12 Georgian Apartments

This Tudor masterpiece was built by Cardinal Thomas Wolsey in 1514, only to be snatched up by Henry VIII (1509–1547). It served as a royal residence from 1528 to 1737, and few places in England exude as much historic atmosphere. Tread the same paths as Elizabeth I (1558–1603), William III (1689–1702), and George II (1727–1760) as you learn about life at court through the centuries.

START: **Hampton Court Station**

1 **Base Court.** Monarchs arrived at Hampton Court via the Thames and entered through the gardens, but visitors today pass through a gatehouse built by Henry VIII for the common folk, and into the Tudor-style courtyard, which is almost exactly as it was when Cardinal Wolsey first built it in 1515. Be sure to examine the turrets surrounding the courtyard, which sport the insignia of Henry VIII and Elizabeth I (who both resided here), as well as numerous carved heads of Roman emperors. 🕐 *10 min.*

2 ★★ **Clock Court.** From the Base Court, pass through the Anne Boleyn Gatehouse (built in the 19th c., long after the beheaded queen's death) and into the Clock Court, which encompasses several architectural styles, ranging from Tudor (the north side) to 18th-century

A costumed guided tour of Hampton Court is wonderful for both kids and adults.

Gothic (the east side). The major attraction is the elaborate Astronomical Clock, built for Henry VIII (note the sun revolving around the earth—the clock was built before Galileo and Copernicus debunked that myth). 🕐 *15 min.*

3 ★★★ kids **Book a Guided Tour.** Stop in at the Information Centre inside the baroque colonnade on the south side of the Clock Court and book a spot on one of the day's costumed guided tours (included with your admission fee). The guides here are knowledgeable and entertaining, and dispense juicy historical tidbits. Kids especially enjoy the experience. You must book in person; do so as soon as you get to the palace, as space on these tours is limited. If you have a choice, opt for the tour of the Henry VIII State Apartments or the King's Apartments. Self-guided palace audio tours are also available (and free). 🕐 *10 min.*

4 ★★★ **Henry VIII State Apartments.** Even though Sir

Hampton Court's famous Astronomical Clock.

Christopher Wren modified some of them, these rooms represent the best examples of Tudor style in England. Don't miss the elaborately gilded ceiling of the **Chapel Royal,** a still-functioning church where Henry was informed of the "misconduct" of his adulterous fifth wife, Catherine Howard, and later married wife number six, Catherine Parr. Right off the chapel is the **Haunted Gallery,** where Howard's ghost reportedly still pleads for her life. The **Watching Chamber,** where senior courtiers would dine, is the only one of Henry VIII's many English estate rooms in something close to its original form (the fireplace and stained glass are not originals). Also impressive is the **Great Hall,** with a set of tapestries (real gold and silver thread) that cost Henry as much as his naval fleet. ⏱ *45 min.*

5 ★★ **Tudor Kitchens.** At its peak, Hampton Court's kitchen staff catered two meals a day to a household of 800. Once the palace lost its popularity with the royal set, the 50-room kitchens were converted into apartments. They were restored in 1991. The enormity of the labor needed to feed the household here

The Chapel Royal is renowned for its gilt ceiling.

The Tudor kitchens, restored to look as they did during the reign of Henry VIII.

is best experienced in the appropriately named **Great Kitchens.** In a small hatchway just outside them are the intriguing **Dressers,** where servants would "dress" and garnish platters sent up to the senior courtiers (check out the marzipan on the table—it's been painted with real gold). ⏱ *45 min.*

The atmospheric **6** ★ kids **Privy Kitchen Coffee Shop** offers a Tudor-style atmosphere (think wooden tables and 16th-century-style chandeliers) along with decent pastries, light lunches, and afternoon tea. *$.*

7 ★ **The Queen's State Apartments.** The rooms in this section of the palace generally appear as they were used by Queen Caroline, wife of George II, from 1716 to 1737. As you climb the frescoed **Staircase,** note Caroline's and George's monograms in the corners of the ceiling. Most impressive is the ornate **State Bedchamber,** one of the only rooms with all of its original furnishings and tapestries (including the heavily draped 18th-c. bed). The **Gallery** was actually built for Queen Mary II (1689–84), and displays top-notch pieces of delftware and Chinese ceramics. ⏱ *25 min.*

8 ★★★ **The South Gardens.**
The palace's most impressive gardens are home to William III's **Privy Garden,** with its elaborate baroque ironwork screen; the box-hedged **Knot Garden,** which resembles a traditional Tudor garden; and the lovely sunken **Pond Gardens,** which were originally ponds where the palace's fish were kept before delivery to the kitchens. Don't skip Mantegna's *Triumph of Caesar,* a series of nine paintings housed in the Lower Orangery (a re-creation of Palace San Sebastiano in Mantua), which are among the most important works of the Italian Renaissance. 🕐 40 min.

9 ★★ **kids The Northern Gardens.** Renowned for their spring bulbs, the Northern Gardens are also where you'll find the palace's famous **Hedge Maze,** whose labyrinthine paths cover nearly a half-mile. Planted in 1702, the maze has trapped many a visitor in its clutches. When you do escape, stroll the adjacent **Tiltyard,** where you'll find several smaller gardens, as well as the only surviving tiltyard tower (used to seat spectators at tournaments) built by Henry VIII. 🕐 30–45 min.

10 ★ **The Tiltyard Café** offers well-priced sandwiches, salads, afternoon teas, and light meals in a slightly upscale setting. If the weather's good, try to sit on the outdoor terrace. You can also picnic on the grass around the cafe, or on the benches in the Clock Court. *$.*

Lose yourself in the tall greenery of the Hedge Maze.

The king's Privy Garden in full bloom.

11 ★★★ **The King's Apartments.** These baroque rooms (among the finest of their kind) were designed by Christopher Wren for William III (1689–1702), who did more to shape the palace than any other monarch, though he died shortly after moving in. The apartments were badly damaged in a 1986 fire (you can still see scorch marks on the ceiling in the **Privy Chamber**), but have been fully restored. All the rooms in this wing are impressive, but a few have notable features. The **Guard Chamber** features a spectacular collection of nearly 3,000 weapons; the **Presence Chamber** has an exquisite rock-crystal chandelier; the **Private Dining Room** has a reproduction of the king's gold-plated dining service (strictly for show); and the **Great Bedchamber** (ceremonial only—the king slept elsewhere) is loaded with gilded furniture, priceless tapestries, and a magnificent red-velvet canopy bed. 🕐 1 hr.

The Queen's Bedchamber is one of the highlights of the Georgian Rooms.

⓬ ★★ **Georgian Apartments.** The private apartments of George II and Queen Caroline still look as they did in 1737, when Caroline died and the royal court left the palace behind forever. The **Presence Chamber** of the 10-year-old Duke of Cumberland (the king's second son) is the only room at the palace that's fully paneled, gilded, and painted. Only a portion of the ceiling of the **Wolsey Closet** is from the Tudor era, though the ceiling is decorated in the Renaissance style. The state bed in the **Queen's Bedchamber** is a reproduction. If the king and queen wanted to sleep together in privacy (which was no mean feat for the royal couple), it was to this room they retired, thanks to a rather sophisticated door lock. ⏱ *45 min.*

Practical Matters

Hampton Court Palace (☎ 0844/482-7777; www.hrp.org.uk) is located in Molesey, Surrey, 21km (13 miles) west of London. Take a train out of London's Waterloo Station to Hampton Court Station; when you exit the station, turn right and follow the signs to the palace, a 10-minute walk away.

Admission to the palace and gardens costs £13 adults, £6.65 kids 5 to 16, £11 seniors and students, £37 family (2 adults, 3 kids). To avoid waiting in lines, and to obtain a £1 discount per ticket, book your tickets on the website (tickets are valid for 1 week from the time of order). Visa and MasterCard are accepted. Tickets are mailed to you or may be picked up at the Prepaid Ticket kiosk on the right side as you face the main ticket booth. The admission fee also includes a free self-guided audio tour; inquire at the Information Centre inside the Clock Court (see ❸).

The palace is open daily 10am to 6pm from April to October (the best time to visit); daily 10am to 4:30pm from November to March. The gardens are open 7am until dusk. Closed December 24, 25, and 26. Arrive at opening time to beat the crowds. ●

The West Front entrance at Hampton Court Palace.

Chelsea

Previous page: Chelsea Royal Hospital.

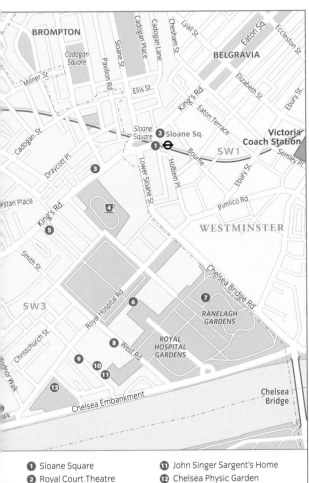

1. Sloane Square
2. Royal Court Theatre
3. King's Road
4. Patisserie Valerie
5. Royal Avenue
6. Chelsea Royal Hospital
7. Ranelagh Gardens
8. National Army Museum
9. Oscar Wilde's Home
10. Augustus John's Studio
11. John Singer Sargent's Home
12. Chelsea Physic Garden
13. George Eliot's Home
14. Dante Gabriel Rossetti's Home
15. Albert Bridge
16. Carlyle Mansions
17. Statue of Sir Thomas More
18. Chelsea Old Church
19. Thomas Carlyle's House
20. Leigh Hunt's Home

Since the 16th century, when Henry VIII and Thomas More built country manors on its bucolic Thames riverbanks, Chelsea has had a long tradition of eccentricity, aristocracy, and artisanship. Home to some of the most picturesque buildings in London, this posh district is one of my favorite spots for a stroll. Keep an eye peeled for blue plaques affixed to the local houses; they tell the story of the many leading figures of English culture who once called this neighborhood home. START: **Sloane Square Tube Station**

① ★★ Sloane Square.
Physician Sir Hans Sloane (1660–1753), who helped found the British Museum and at one point owned most of Chelsea, is the namesake of this attractive square. In addition to his educational and medical achievements, Sloane discovered the chocolate recipe that became the basis of the Cadbury empire. *Intersection of Sloane St. & King's Rd.*

Fountain in Sloane Square.

② ★★ Royal Court Theatre.
This restored theater, originally built in 1888, is famous for showcasing playwrights such as George Bernard Shaw, John Osborne, and Harold Pinter. Nowadays, the work of today's most promising dramatists is performed on the two stages. *A*

King's Road, Chelsea's major thoroughfare, is loaded with ritzy shops.

few steps to the right of the Sloane Sq. Tube exit. ☎ 0207/565-5000. www.royalcourttheatre.com.

③ ★★★ King's Road.
Chelsea's main road was once an exclusive royal passage used by Charles II to go from Whitehall to Hampton Court. It was also a favorite route of highwaymen looking to "liberate" some royal goods. An echo of these King's Road robbers can be found in the extortionate prices of the chichi stores that now line this shopping-focused thoroughfare. The area is a favorite of the young and free-spending members of London's upper social strata. *Runs from Sloane Sq. southwest to Putney Bridge.*

The Duke of York Square has a number of good dining spots, but you can't go wrong at **④ ★ Patisserie Valerie.** Hot dishes, salads, and sandwiches are reliably good; and the desserts are killer. Try the oversize croissants for breakfast or a teatime snack. *81 Duke of York Sq. (off King's Rd.). 0207/245-6161. $.*

⑤ ★ Royal Avenue. This small, picturesque road was intended to extend all the way from nearby Chelsea Royal Hospital to Kensington Palace when it was laid out in

1682 by Sir Christopher Wren, but construction was cut short upon the death of its commissioner, Charles II. *Between St. Leonard's Terrace & King's Rd.*

⑥ ★★★ Chelsea Royal Hospital. This Christopher Wren masterpiece, commissioned by Charles II in 1692 as a retirement estate for injured and old soldiers, is home to 400-plus pensioners who still dress in traditional uniforms and offer informative tours of the historic grounds and chapel. It's the site of Chelsea's Flower Show, held every May since 1912. *Royal Hospital Rd.* ☎ *0207/881-0161. Free admission. Guided tours by prior arrangement only. Mon–Sat 10am–noon, 2–4pm; Sun 2–4pm. Church services open to public, Sun 10:30am.*

⑦ ★★ Ranelagh Gardens. Once centered about a large rotunda (demolished in 1805), these gardens (some of the prettiest in London) were a favorite of 18th-century socialites who were occasionally entertained here by a young Mozart. *At Chelsea Royal Hospital. Free admission. Mon–Sat 10am–noon, 2–4pm; Sun 2–4pm.*

⑧ ★★ National Army Museum. Home of the Duke of Wellington's shaving mirror and Florence Nightingale's lamp, this

A plaque marks the site of Oscar Wilde's Chelsea home.

One of Chelsea Royal Hospital's pensioners.

museum follows the history of Britain's fighting forces from the Middle Ages to the present. *Royal Hospital Rd.* ☎ *0207/730-0717. www.national-army-museum.ac.uk. Free admission. Daily 10am–5:30pm.*

⑨ ★★ Oscar Wilde's Home. The eccentricities of Oscar and his wife Constance (they lived here 1885–1895) were well known to neighbors, who would often see them on the street dressed in velvet (him) and a huge Gainsborough hat (her). Street boys would shout, "'Ere comes 'Amlet and Ophelia!" The house is not open to the public. *34 Tite St.*

⑩ ★ Augustus John's Studio. A renowned Welsh painter (1878–1961), John was one of Chelsea's most illustrious artists. His insightful portraits and landscapes made him famous, while his bohemian lifestyle and love affairs (including one with the mother of James Bond creator Ian Fleming) earned him notoriety. *33 Tite St.*

The Best Neighborhood Walks

Gardeners will delight in Chelsea Physic Garden's bounty of herbs and plants.

⓫ ★★ **John Singer Sargent's Home.** The renowned American portraitist of the high and mighty lived and worked at this address (the former abode of the equally famous artist James McNeill Whistler) from 1901 until his death in 1925. *31 Tite St.*

⓬ ★★ **Chelsea Physic Garden.** This garden was established in 1673 by the Apothecaries' Company to cultivate medicinal plants and herbs. Cotton seeds from the garden were sent to America in 1732, and slavery became their eventual harvest. *66 Royal Hospital Rd.* ☎ *0207/352-5646. www.chelseaphysicgarden.co.uk. Admission £7 adults, £4 kids 5–15. Mid-Mar to Nov Wed–Fri noon–5pm,* *Sun noon–6pm. See website for special events.*

⓭ ★ **George Eliot's Home.** The famous Victorian novelist, born Mary Ann Evans in 1819, moved into this house with her new and much younger husband, John Cross, only a few months before her death in December 1880. *4 Cheyne Walk.*

⓮ ★ **Dante Gabriel Rossetti's Home.** The eccentric pre-Raphaelite poet and painter (1828–82) moved here in 1862 after the death of his wife. He kept a menagerie of many exotic animals, including kangaroos, a white bull, peacocks, and a wombat that inspired his friend, Lewis Carroll, to create the Dormouse in *Alice in Wonderland. 16 Cheyne Walk.*

⓯ ★★★ **Albert Bridge.** Designed by R. M. Ordish, this picturesque suspension bridge linking Battersea and Chelsea was completed in 1873. Conservationists kept the bridge from destruction in the 1950s. In 1973, the cast-iron structure had new supports installed so it could cope with the rigors of modern traffic. The sight of seagulls and sparrows wheeling above the span is part of its considerable charm.

The Albert Bridge spans the Thames, linking Battersea with Chelsea.

16 ★ Carlyle Mansions. Henry James (1843–1916), the great American novelist *(Portrait of a Lady)*, was sick in bed inside his riverview flat when he was honored for his work (and for taking British citizenship) with the Order of the British Empire. Only a few weeks later, the writer drew his last breath here in his beautiful and chic apartment house. *Cheyne Walk.*

17 ★★ Statue of Sir Thomas More. Despite his long friendship with Henry VIII, Lord Chancellor Thomas More (1478–1535) refused to accept Henry as head of the Church of England after the king's notorious break with the Roman Catholic Church. More paid for his religious convictions with his life—he was tried and subsequently beheaded for treason in 1535. In 1935, the Roman Catholic Church canonized him as Saint Thomas More, the patron saint of lawyers and politicians. *Old Church St.*

18 ★★ Chelsea Old Church. A church has stood on this site since 1157. Though the structure suffered serious damage during the Blitz, it has since been rebuilt and restored. Sir Thomas More worshiped here (he built the South Chapel in 1528), and it was also the setting of Henry VIII's secret marriage to third wife Jane Seymour in 1536. *64 Cheyne*

The Victorian home of historian Thomas Carlyle has been remarkably preserved.

This statue of Sir Thomas More stands just outside Chelsea Old Church.

Walk. ☎ 0207/795-1019. www.chelseaoldchurch.org.uk.

19 ★★★ Thomas Carlyle's House. The famous Scottish historian (1795–1881) and his wife, Jane, entertained friends Dickens and Chopin in this remarkably well-preserved Victorian home. It was here that the "Sage of Chelsea" finished his important *History of the French Revolution. 24 Cheyne Row.* ☎ 0207/352-7087. www.nationaltrust.org.uk. Admission £3.70 adults, £1.80 kids 5–16. Apr–Oct Wed–Fri 2–5pm, Sat–Sun 11am–5pm.

20 ★ Leigh Hunt's Home. From 1833 to 1840, the noted poet and essayist (a friend of Byron and Keats) lived here, and was well known for pestering neighbors for loans. His wife infuriated Jane Carlyle with her incessant borrowing of household items. *22 Upper Cheyne Row.*

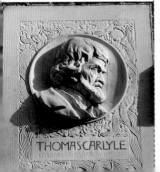

THOMAS CARLYLE

Hampstead

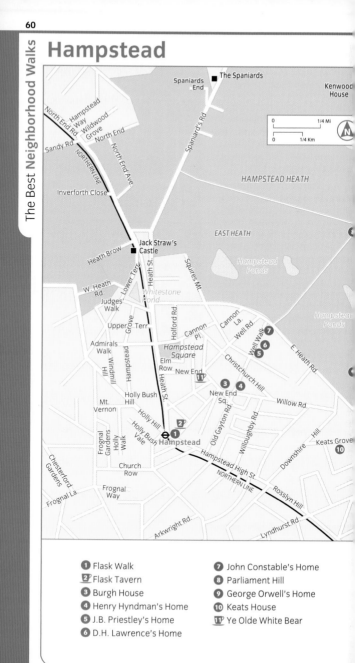

1 Flask Walk
2 Flask Tavern
3 Burgh House
4 Henry Hyndman's Home
5 J.B. Priestley's Home
6 D.H. Lawrence's Home

7 John Constable's Home
8 Parliament Hill
9 George Orwell's Home
10 Keats House
11 Ye Olde White Bear

Hampstead first became popular for its fresh air and salubrious waters during the Great Plague of 1665, when well-to-do Londoners bolted from their infected neighborhoods to escape the contagion before they were quarantined with the dying. Today, this village is still a charming refuge, known for its historical buildings, fun shops, and bracing proximity to the Heath, 324 hectares (800 acres) of controlled wilderness and far-reaching views. Come here for a look at a kinder, gentler London. START: **Hampstead Tube Station**

❶ ★ **Flask Walk.** Now a street of expensive homes and chichi shops, Flask Walk was the site of early-18th-century fairs and also home to year-round establishments for drinking and gambling—all built to entertain the crush of Londoners escaping the fetid city streets for Hampstead's fresh air. The street was named for a now-defunct tavern that bottled the village's pure water and sold it throughout London.

The three-room ❷ ★★ **Flask Tavern,** a Victorian pub built in 1874 on the site of the old Thatched House Pub, is cozy in the winter thanks to its cast-iron fireplace, and offers a few outdoor tables in good weather. It serves reliable pub grub, and is worth visiting for its appealing atmosphere. *14 Flask Walk.* ☎ *0207/435-4580. MC, V. $$.*

Flask Walk in the village of Hampstead.

Explore the local history of Hampstead at Burgh House.

❸ ★ **Burgh House.** Built in 1704, this restored Queen Anne structure, the former home of spa physician Dr. William Gibbon, now houses a museum that specializes in the local history of Hampstead and features a permanent exhibit on the painter John Constable, who lived nearby.

New End Sq. ☎ *0207/431-0144.*
www.burghhouse.org.uk. Free
admission. Wed–Sun noon–5pm.

❹ ★ Henry Hyndman's Home.

A journalist, politician, and public speaker, Hyndman (1842–1921) founded the Social Democratic Federation, England's first socialist party, in 1881. He lived in this house until his death in 1921. *13 Well Walk.*

❺ ★ J. B. Priestley's Home.

One of England's most prolific men of letters, Priestley (1894–1984) was an essayist, playwright, biographer, historian, and social commentator who refused a knighthood and peerage. He lived in this Queen Anne–style house from 1929 to 1931. *28 Well Walk.*

❻ ★★ D. H. Lawrence's Home.

During World War I, Lawrence (1885–1930) made his home here after being kicked out of Cornwall when his wife was unjustly accused of being a German spy. He left in 1919 for Italy, where he wrote his most famous novel, *Lady Chatterley's Lover,* in 1928. The book was banned in England on charges of indecency and wasn't published there uncensored until 1960. *32 Well Walk.*

Stand atop Parliament Hill for some of the loveliest views of London.

The greenery of Hampstead Heath has inspired many a writer and artist.

❼ ★★ John Constable's Home.

The well-known British landscape painter and portraitist resided here from 1827 until his death in 1837. It was in his many studies of nearby Hampstead Heath that Constable mastered the depiction of weather in landscapes, tirelessly painting the same scene under different climatic conditions. *40 Well Walk.*

❽ ★★★ Parliament Hill.

Guy Fawkes and his co-conspirators in the 1605 Gunpowder Plot to blow up Parliament planned to view the aftermath of their handiwork from this vantage point. It's the best place to watch the fireworks staged every November 5 to commemorate the plot. A map on the site identifies the buildings in the distance. *Inside Hampstead Heath.*

❾ ★★ George Orwell's Home.

The author of *Animal Farm, 1984,* and the classic book on London, *Down and Out in Paris and London,* wrote the satirical *Keep the Aspidistra Flying* in a backroom on the second floor of this house. He lived here for only 6 months in 1936 while working part-time at

Booklover's Corner, a small bookshop on South End Green (it's now a pizza shop). *77 Parliament Hill St.*

⑩ ★★★ **Keats House.** It was in this house (built by combining two Regency cottages), in 1819, that Keats wrote his famous *Ode to a Nightingale, Ode on a Grecian Urn,* and *Ode to Psyche*. It was also while living here that Keats fell in love with next-door neighbor Fanny Browne, his eventual fiancée (and the muse behind many of his best works). The Romantic poet lived in this house from 1818 until 1820, when he traveled to Italy, where he died of tuberculosis only a few months later. *Keats Grove.* ☎ *0207/435-2062. www.cityoflondon.gov.uk/keats. At press time, Keats House was closed for a major renovation; for up-to-date visitor information, check the website.*

The poet John Keats wrote his famous *Ode on a Grecian Urn* while living in this Hampstead house.

With dark woodcarvings, fine furniture, and photos of the area's celebs on the walls, ⑪ ★★ **Ye Olde White Bear** manages to project the atmosphere of a country village pub, even though it serves sophisticated Londoners and has urban prices. *Corner of Well Rd. and New End Rd.* ☎ *0207/435-3758. MC, V. $.*

The Loos of London

One of London's greatest public conveniences is the ubiquity of public lavatories, making the city far friendlier to the strolling visitor than, say, New York. Public restrooms are usually very clean and stocked with toilet paper. These oases for the visitor used to cost 1p, hence the local euphemism for nature's call, "spending a penny." Today, you've got to spend 20p (50p on Oxford St.), at either the old-fashioned tiled below-ground Gents' and Ladies' rooms, or the free-standing metal kiosks that get a complete hose-down and cleaning automatically after each use. Have a 20p or 50p coin handy at all times, but if you're stuck, you can usually find a free loo at a public library, park, or museum; and you can thank globalization for the restrooms at Starbucks or McDonald's. In a pinch, you can also try a pub or restaurant, though I'd buy a little something to become a customer first. You could try a department store or hotel, too.

The Best Neighborhood Walks

Mayfair

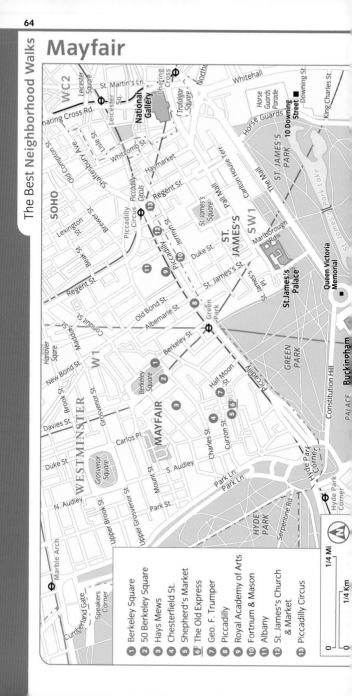

1. Berkeley Square
2. 50 Berkeley Square
3. Hays Mews
4. Chesterfield St.
5. Shepherd's Market
6. The Old Express
7. Geo. F. Trumper
8. Piccadilly
9. Royal Academy of Arts
10. Fortnum & Mason
11. Albany
12. St. James's Church & Market
13. Piccadilly Circus

For over three centuries, Mayfair has been an exclusive neighborhood of the aristocracy, who used to live in grand style inside elegant mansions run by armies of servants. Most of these urban palaces have been destroyed over the years, but enough survive to make a walk through Mayfair a fascinating glimpse into how London's rich lived—and often still live. This walk focuses on the southern part of Mayfair. START: **Green Park Tube Station**

Berkeley Square's west side is home to several picturesque town houses.

❶ ★ **Berkeley Square.** Immortalized in song and associated with nightingales (nowhere to be found today), this square was once the most aristocratic spot in London. Notables who've called the square home include Prime Ministers Winston Churchill (who lived at No. 48 as a boy) and George Canning (who resided briefly at No. 50; see ❷). Its modern east side, loaded with undistinguished office buildings, doesn't bear looking at. Keep your eyes on the lovely old houses on the west side. (Lansdowne House on the southwest corner was designed by famed Scottish architect Robert Adam.) And check out

the maple-like plane trees that surround the square; they were planted in 1789 and are among the oldest in the city.

❷ ★★ **50 Berkeley Square.** This Georgian-style building (now home to a respectable bookshop) was known as the "most haunted house in London" in the 19th century, when sightings of a bewigged man and sounds of an unearthly nature kept the house untenanted. Though strange happenings here have been reported in recent years by visitors, the worst of the haunting seems to have taken place in Victorian days, when an evil presence in what was known as the "haunted room" so terrified a visitor, he threw himself out the window and was impaled on the railings below.

❸ ★ **Hays Mews.** There were once mews—garages with carriages and horses on the lower floor, and living quarters for the groom and coachmen upstairs—like this one found throughout London. Today, most mews have been converted into expensive homes, but some lucky owners still use them for their cars. *To the left of the Coach & Horses Pub on Hays Mews.*

❹ ★★ **Chesterfield Street.** This is the least altered Georgian street in Mayfair and a great place to soak up the neighborhood's atmosphere. Its former inhabitants include historians Edward Gibbon and Edmund Burke. As you stroll along its sidewalks, you'll see plaques identifying the former homes of Regency dandy Beau Brummell and writer Somerset Maugham.

5 ★★★ Shepherd's Market. In the mid–18th century, developer Edward Shepherd bought the land on which the riotous May Fair (the neighborhood's namesake) took place each spring. Subsequent development put an end to that often-outlawed orgy. The result was much what you see now: charming yet humble buildings from the days when the market was the hub of the servant classes in Mayfair. Where once you would find useful emporia selling meat and groceries, today you'll find upscale chocolate shops and jewelry stores.

A favorite with the locals, **6 ★★ The Old Express** serves great traditional English food such as fish and chips, sausage and mash, and cottage pie. *30 Shepherd Market.* ☎ *0207/499-1299. $$.*

7 ★★★ Geo. F. Trumper. Where else can you get a shave with a straight razor and shaving brush these days? This English institution opened in 1875, and is so authentically old-fashioned that you half expect to be told not to touch anything. Even if you don't need a shave or toiletries, do have a look at this wonderful shop. *9 Curzon St.* ☎ *0207/499-1850. www. trumpers.com.*

8 ★★ Piccadilly. The name Piccadilly is said to have come from the word "picadil," a stiff collar manufactured by a tailor of the early 17th century who bought a great parcel of land on which he built a grand home. Lest the upstart forget his humble beginnings, it was sneeringly referred to as "Piccadilly Hall." In the 18th and

Carved classical heads mark the facade of the Ritz hotel on Piccadilly, a street loaded with interesting architectural styles and features.

19th centuries, many great mansions were built along the street facing Green Park. Head east on Piccadilly so you can admire the elaborate gates surrounding Green Park and the carved classical-style heads on the Parisian-inspired facade of the Ritz hotel.

9 ★★★ Royal Academy of Arts. Burlington House, built in the 1660s, was a magnificent estate purchased by the government in 1854 to house England's oldest arts society. The Royal Academy mounts popular exhibitions in this small but lovely space. The permanent collection includes one of only four Michelangelo sculptures found outside of Italy. *Burlington House, Piccadilly.* ☎ *0207/300-8000. www.royalacademy.org.uk.*

10 ★★ Fortnum & Mason. This famous partnership began in 1705, when shop owner Hugh Mason let a room to William Fortnum, a footman for Queen Anne at the Palace of St. James. The enterprising Fortnum "recycled" candle ends from the palace (the Queen required fresh candles nightly), and sold them to Mason. From this humble beginning, Fortnum & Mason grew to rule Britannia (or at least, Piccadilly), with one of the earliest of globally recognized brand names. For an authentic (and pricey) afternoon tea, try the St. James Restaurant on the fourth floor. *181 Piccadilly.*

⑪ ★★ **Albany.** Built in the 1770s by architect William Chambers for Lord Melbourne, this grand Georgian building was turned into a residence for gentlemen in 1802. Since then, many poets (Lord Byron), authors (Graham Greene), and playwrights have all called this prime Piccadilly patch home. *At Albany Court off Piccadilly.*

⑫ ★★★ **St. James's Church & Market.** This unprepossessing redbrick church is one of Christopher Wren's simplest, said by Charles Dickens to be "not one of the master's happiest efforts." The poet William Blake was baptized here, as was William Pitt, the first earl of Chatham, who became England's youngest prime minister at age 24. You are welcome to enter and sit in its quiet interior, or enjoy the free (donations desperately needed) lunchtime recitals. There's a market in the forecourt Tuesday through Saturday, featuring crafts, clothes, and collectibles. *197 Piccadilly.*
☎ *0207/734-4511. www. st-james-piccadilly.org.*

⑬ ★★ **Piccadilly Circus.** London's answer to New York's Times

Piccadilly Circus, located in the heart of Mayfair, is awash in neon at night.

Square was the first place in the city to sport electrical signage, and it still dazzles the eye at night. The word *circus* refers to a circular juncture at an intersection of streets, and the plaza was built in 1819 to connect two of London's major shopping streets: Regent Street and Piccadilly. The statue of Eros on the central island of Piccadilly Circus is a favorite meeting place and hangout. Officially, it's called the Shaftesbury Memorial Fountain, designed in 1893 by Alfred Gilbert in memory of the seventh earl of Shaftesbury, a venerable Victorian philanthropist. It was supposed to be a statue of The Angel of Christian Charity, but has always been known as Eros.

The statue of Eros on the central island of Piccadilly Circus.

Whitehall

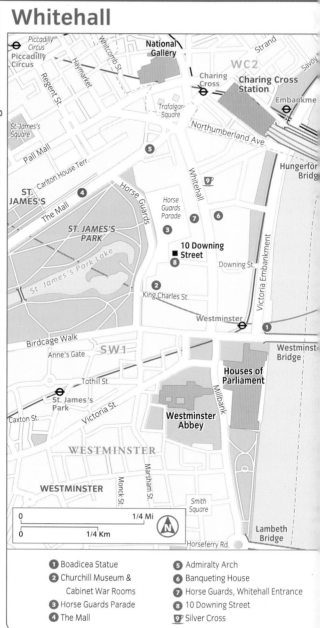

1 Boadicea Statue
2 Churchill Museum & Cabinet War Rooms
3 Horse Guards Parade
4 The Mall
5 Admiralty Arch
6 Banqueting House
7 Horse Guards, Whitehall Entrance
8 10 Downing Street
9 Silver Cross

Once the site of the vast Palace of Whitehall—London's chief royal residence from 1530 to 1698—this area is now a dignified neighborhood of government buildings whose grand architecture confers a certain beauty to the dull business of bureaucracy. If the United Kingdom can be said to have a political center, then Whitehall is it. This walk works best in the morning; try to time your arrival at Horse Guards Parade at 11am to see the Changing of the Guard. START: **Westminster Tube Station**

1 ★★ **Boadicea Statue.** A tall and ferocious queen of the Iceni tribe of East Anglia, Boadicea waged battle against Britain's 1st-century Roman invaders, nailing captured soldiers to trees and flaying them alive. In A.D. 61, her forces killed 70,000 Romans and temporarily retook Londinium before they were thoroughly defeated by the Roman army. The queen (whose name means victorious) became a heroic figure of Victorian England. This statue by Thomas Thornycroft was erected in 1902. *Bridge St. & Victoria Embankment.*

2 ★★ kids **Churchill Museum & Cabinet War Rooms.** Winston Churchill directed World War II from this underground shelter as German bombs rained down on London. The basements of the Civil Service buildings along King Charles Street were converted in 1938, with an area of roughly 1.2 hectares (3 acres) redesigned to house a hospital, a cafeteria, sleeping quarters, and even a shooting range in the low, cramped rooms. After the war, the

William Churchill's desk inside the Cabinet War Rooms.

area was locked and left untouched until Churchill's quarters were turned into a museum in 1981; all the items you see are the genuine article. *Clive Steps, King Charles St.* ☎ *0207/930-6961. http://cwr.iwm.org.uk.*

3 ★★ kids **Horse Guards Parade.** London's largest open space dates back to 1745 and offers excellent views of Whitehall's impressive architecture. It's best known as the site for the annual Trooping the Colour. Every day at 11am (10am on Sun) there's a much mellower (and less crowded) Changing of the Guard than you'll find at Buckingham Palace (p 22, **3**). *Horseguards Rd.*

4 ★★ **The Mall.** This thoroughfare—running west from Buckingham Palace (see p 45, **1**) to Trafalgar Square (see p 22, **6**)—was created in 1660 as an annex to St. James's Park for the gallants to play the popular game of *paille mall* (a precursor to croquet). In the early 18th century it was a fashionable promenade for the beau monde, and in 1903 it was redesigned as a processional route for royal occasions. When foreign heads of state visit the queen, the Mall is decked out in the Union Jack and the flags of the visitor's country. *Between Buckingham Palace & Admiralty Arch.*

5 ★ **Admiralty Arch.** Built in 1910, this quintuple-arched building looks west to the grand statue of Queen Victoria in front of Buckingham Palace. The central gates are

The Banqueting House, the last surviving remnant of Whitehall Palace.

for ceremonial use, opening only to let a royal procession pass. Note the adorable little ships sitting atop some of the nearby street lamps in a nod to the Old Admiralty Offices for which the arch was named.

6 ★★★ **Banqueting House.** All that remains of Whitehall Palace is this hall, completed in 1622 by Inigo Jones. The city's first Renaissance-style construction is best known for its glorious Rubens-painted ceiling—commissioned by Charles I (1600–49), who used the building for parties and greeting foreign delegations. The allegorical ceiling, equating the Stuart kings with the gods, may have gone to Charles's head—his belief in the divine right of kings led directly to the removal of that head when he was executed for treason in 1649 on a scaffold just outside the hall. Whitehall. ☎ 0844/482-7777. www.hrp.org.uk. Adults £4.50, kids & seniors £3.50. Mon–Sat 10am–5pm.

7 **Horse Guards, Whitehall Entrance.** Just across from the Banqueting House is another entrance to Horse Guards Parade guarded by two mounted soldiers in ceremonial garb, who appear to do nothing but provide good photo ops for visitors. Go through the gates and have a look through the arched tunnel, framing a beautiful view of St. James's Park.

8 ★ **10 Downing Street.** The home address of Britain's prime minister since 1732 is set in a quiet cul-de-sac. The street was open to the public until 1990, when it was blocked off by iron gates for security reasons. There's not much to see now except a lot of security guards giving you the evil eye, though there is a *frisson* of excitement to be had while standing near so much power.

Of the many fine pubs that line Whitehall, my favorite is the 9 **Silver Cross,** which, despite its faux ye olde England decor, is genuinely old (it was granted a brothel license in 1674). It offers good fish and chips, lots of seating, and its own ghost—a young girl in Tudor dress. *33 Whitehall.* ☎ *0207/930-8350. $$.* ●

A sentry and his mount at the Whitehall entrance to Horse Guards Parade.

5 The **Best Shopping**

Shopping Best Bets

Best **Time to Shop**
During the August and January
citywide, month-long sales

Best **Shot at Last Season's
Designer Threads**
★★★ Pandora, *16–22 Cheval Place*
(p 80)

Best **Important Jewelry**
★★★ Ritz Fine Jewelry, *150 Piccadilly (p 82)*

Best **Fun & Vintage Jewelry**
★★ Hirst Antiques, *59 Pembridge
Rd. (p 82)*

Best **Sugar Rush**
★★★ The Chocolate Society, *36
Elizabeth St. (p 80)*

Best **Children's Toy Store**
★★★ Honey Jam, *267 Portobello
Rd. (p 84)*

Best **Place to Score Stuff from
Other People's Attics**
★★★ Grays Antique Market,
58 Davies St. (p 76)

Best **Foot Forward**
★★ The Natural Shoe Store, *21
Neal St. (p 79)*

Best **Historic Bookstore**
★★★ Hatchards, *187 Piccadilly
(p 78)*

Best **Hot-Date Lingerie**
★★ Agent Provocateur, *6 Broadwick St. (p 82)*

Best **Art Supplies**
★★★ Print Gallery Art Shop,
22 Pembridge Rd. (p 84)

Most **Fun Auction House**
★★★ Auction Atrium, *101b Kensington Church St. (p 76)*

Best **of All Worlds**
★★★ General Trading Company,
2 Symons St. (p 81)

Best **Weekend Browsing**
★★★ Portobello Road Market,
Portobello Rd. (p 83)

Best **Everything**
★★★ Selfridges, *400 Oxford St.
(p 80)*

Best **Museum Shop**
★★★ Victoria and Albert
Museum, *Cromwell Rd. (p 83)*

Best **Parfumerie**
★★★ Angela Flanders, *96 Columbia Rd. (p 76)*

*Portobello Road Market is London's most
famous antiques market.*

Knightsbridge Shopping

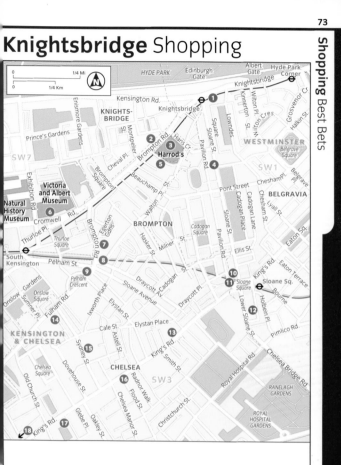

London Shopping

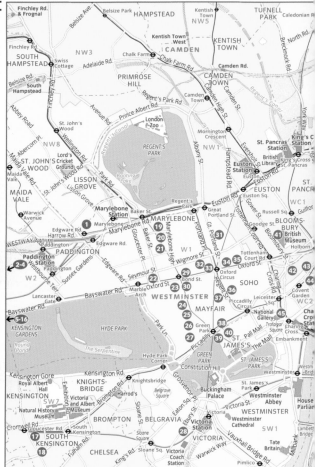

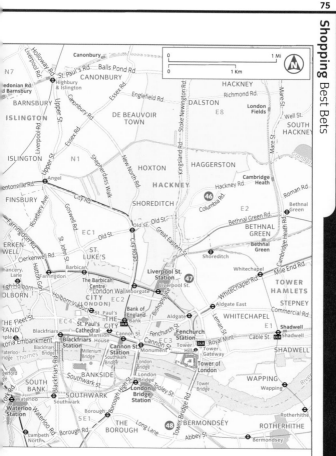

London Shopping A to Z

Antiques & Art Auctions

★★ Alfie's Antique Market

MARYLEBONE   The city's largest collection of dealers—four floors of secondhand knickknacks, plus old fabrics and dresses. *13–25 Church St.* ☎ *0207/723-6066. www.alfies antiques.com. Some dealers take credit cards. Tube: Marylebone or Edgware Rd. Map p 74.*

★★ Antiquarius

CHELSEA   The number of stalls has been reduced, but you're still bound to find both high-end and more affordable silver, antique jewelry, clocks, collectables, and art. *131–141 King's Rd.* ☎ *0207/ 823-3900. Some dealers take credit cards. Tube: Sloane Sq. Map p 73.*

★★★ Arieta Antiques

KENSING-TON   Tiny, and charming, this wonderful curio shop is the rare store where you'll find something unusual that won't blow your budget. *97B Kensington Church St.* ☎ *0207/243-1074. MC, V. Tube: Notting Hill Gate. Map p 74.*

★★★ Auction Atrium

KENSING-TON   This richly filled walk-in shop has a user-friendly bidding Website that offers affordable estate sales and lots of buy-now items at good prices. It's much more fun than the big houses. *101b Kensington Church St.* ☎ *0207/792-9020. www.auction atrium.com. AE, MC, V, PayPal. Tube: Notting Hill Gate. Map p 74.*

★★ Bourbon-Hanby Arcade

CHELSEA   A rather grand collection of antiques stalls featuring upscale estate goods, jewelry, and fine art. *151 Sydney St.* ☎ *0207/352-2106. www.bourbonhanby.co.uk. Some dealers take credit cards. Tube: Sloane Sq. Map p 73.*

★★ Christie's

SOUTH KENSINGTON   Don't be scared off by the cost of

Chelsea's Antiquarius is home to a wide variety of antiques dealers.

the serious treasures—this venerable auction house usually has something for all budgets. *85 Old Brompton Rd.* ☎ *0207/930-6074. www.christies.com. AE, MC, V. Tube: S. Kensington. Map p 74.*

★★★ Grays Antique Market

MAYFAIR   Stalls here sell everything from Art Deco paperweights to antique jewelry to vintage Edwardian toys. *58 Davies St.* ☎ *0207/ 629-7034. www.graysantiques.com. Some dealers take credit cards. Tube: Bond St., Marble Arch. Map p 74.*

★★★ Lev Antiques

KENSINGTON   For fabulous estate jewelry and small, odd whatnots, silver, and art, Lev's is friendly and well priced. *97a Kensington Church St.* ☎ *0207/727-9248. MC, V. Tube: Notting Hill Gate. Map p 74.*

Beauty Products

★★★ Angela Flanders

EAST END   This exclusive shop is well worth the effort it takes to get to the East End on a Sunday (or by appointment). Flanders' bespoke, signature scents have a devoted clientele. *96 Columbia Rd.* 📞 *0207/739-7555. www.angelaflanders-perfumer.com. MC, V. Tube: Old St. Map p 75.*

★★★ **Geo. F. Trumper** MAYFAIR An essential shop for the well-groomed man, the woman who wants a great gift for her guy, or anyone interested in high-quality toiletries and accessories. *9 Curzon St.* 📞 *0207/499-1850. www.trumpers.com. AE, MC, V. Tube: Gloucester Rd. Map p 74.*

★★ **Miller Harris** MAYFAIR Trained in Grasse, France, Lyn Harris has created a global brand of sexy and elegant scents of the finest quality. The packaging is just as intriguing as the perfumes, lotions, and candles for sale. *21 Bruton St.* 📞 *0207/629-7750. www.millerharris.com. AE, DC, MC, V. Tube Green Park. Map p 74.*

★★★ **Pout** COVENT GARDEN This shop is a makeup junkie's favorite

fix: It's got everything you need—or crave. Their own very chic product line is a favorite of celebs. *32 Shelton St.* 📞 *0207/379-0379. AE, MC, V. Tube: Covent Garden. Map p 74.*

★★ **Screen Face** COVENT GARDEN Even if you're not in the market for a special-effects bruise kit, you'll be knocked out by the range and variety of makeup, accessories, and skin goods at this favorite of pro makeup artists. *48 Monmouth St.* 📞 *0207/836-3955. www.screenface.com. MC, V. Tube: Covent Garden. Map p 74.*

★★ **Space NK** NOTTING HILL This popular English chain sells many boutique-style lines of makeup, creams, fragrances, and decadently scented candles. *127–131 Westbourne Grove.* 📞 *0207/727-8063. www.spacenk.co.uk. AE, MC, V. Tube: Notting Hill Gate. Map p 74.*

Books & Stationery
★★★ **The Book Warehouse** NOTTING HALL Great prices on a wide variety of remainder books, as

VAT (Value Added Tax)

The U.K. levies a crushing 17.5% Value Added Tax (VAT) on all non-essential goods. (VAT is included in the price tag, unless it clearly states "plus VAT.") If you have your purchases sent home, you can avoid the VAT, but you must pay shipping and duty fees. Most shops will help you get a partial refund of the VAT (usually 13%–15%) if you spend a certain amount, usually at least £50. Ask for a VAT form when you pay for an item and have it filled out in the shop—forms must be validated by the seller for you to claim your refund! When you get to the airport, present your form, passport, and purchases—do not pack them in your checked luggage—to the Customs agency for certification. Once your papers have been stamped, you can get a cash refund from one of the agencies at the airport (minus a service charge), or you can mail in the forms to get a cash or credit card refund. The process is a hassle and worth going through only for high-ticket items. For more information, go to **www.hmce.gov.uk** or **www.visitbritain.com**.

Hatchards sells a wide variety of books, but is best known for its royalty section.

well as tons of fun and quirky gift items, art supplies, toys, games, and London-themed items. *123 Gloucester Rd.* ☎ *0207/370-3503. MC, V. Tube: Gloucester Rd. Map p 74.*

★★★ **Daunt Books** MARYLEBONE One of the few independent bookshops left in London, with an excellent travel section and the latest U.K. fiction. Peaceful atmosphere for browsing. *183 Marylebone High St.* ☎ *0207/224-2295. www.daunt books.co.uk. MC, V. Tube: Baker St. Map p 74.*

★★★ **Gloucester Road Book Store** KENSINGTON   Good prices on secondhand books that have been carefully culled by the knowledgeable staff. Check out the coffee mugs imprinted with old Penguin book covers. *123 Gloucester Rd.* ☎ *0207/370-3503. MC, V. Tube: Gloucester Rd. Map p 74.*

★★★ **Hatchards** PICCADILLY This home for discerning bibliophiles has been in business since 1797. It's tops for books on royalty. *187 Piccadilly.* ☎ *0207/439-9921. www.hatchards.co.uk. AE, DC, MC, V. Tube: Green Park. Map p 74.*

★★★ **Smythson of Bond Street** MAYFAIR   This expensive and exclusive stationer caters to generations of posh Londoners, who would feel naked without a Smythson appointment diary. *40*

New Bond St. ☎ *0207/629-8558. www.smythson.com. AE, DC, MC, V. Tube: Bond St. Map p 74.*

★★★ **Talking Book Shop** MARYLEBONE   Gob-smacking selection of unabridged classics, nonfiction published only in the U.K., and kids' lit for all ages. There are CDs and tapes, too. *11 Wigmore St.* ☎ *0207/491-4117. www.talking books.co.uk. MC, V. Tube: Bond St. Map p 74.*

Clothing & Shoes
★★ **The Antique Clothing Shop** NOTTING HILL   Lots of great old glad rags, plus rarer work get-ups from your great-grandmother's day. *282 Portobello Rd.* ☎ *0208/ 964-4830. AE. Tube: Ladbroke Grove. Map p 74.*

★★ **Browns** MAYFAIR   The best place in town for up-to-the-minute fashions, including a discriminating collection of hip designers. Keep your eyes peeled for sales. *23–27 S. Moulton St.* ☎ *0207/514-0000. www.brownsfashion.com. AE, MC, V. Tube: Bond St. Map p 74.*

★★ **Catwalk** MARYLEBONE There's always an excellent chance

The immense Topshop sells a versatile lineup of fashion for women.

For high-style home furnishings and gift items, head for The Conran Shop.

of getting some designer clothes and shoes at this "nearly new" shop, crammed with top labels that are priced to move. *52 Blandford St.* ☎ *0207/935-1052. MC, V. Tube: Baker. Map p 74.*

★★★ **Coco Ribbon** NOTTING HILL Besides their own brand of underwear, this boutique carries the latest clothes and accessories from Antique Batik and others, plus Repetto shoes. *21 Kensington Park Rd.* ☎ *0207/229-4904. www.cocoribbon.com. AE, MC, V. Tube: Ladbroke Grove or Notting Hill Gate. Map p 74.*

★★★ **The Cross** HOLLAND PARK Fashionistas in the know flock here for Missoni, Johnny Loves Rosie, Alice Lee, and other designers. You'll also find some housewares and surprisingly witty children's gifts. *141 Portland Rd.* ☎ *0207/727-6760. AE, MC, V. Tube: Holland Park. Map p 74.*

★★ **Dover Street Market** MAYFAIR Resoundingly and expensively cutting edge, the DSM encompasses four floors of top fashion: Commes des Garcons shares space with Zandra Rhodes, Azzedine Alaia, L'Wren Scott, Boudicca, and the latest catwalk stars. *17–18 Dover St.* ☎ *0207/518-0680. www.doverstreetmarket.com. AE, MC, V. Tube: Green Park. Map p 74.*

★★★ **Jimmy Choo** SOUTH KENSINGTON This London designer–turned–global brand pops up on the well-tended feet of Oscar contenders and well-kept mistresses. You'll pay dearly for a pair. *169 Draycott Ave.* ☎ *0207/584-6111. www.jimmychoo. com. AE, MC, V. Tube: S. Kensington. Map p 73.*

★★ **L.K. Bennett** SOUTH KENSINGTON Leave the clothes on the racks, but do step into the shoes. Boots are plentiful, and there are scads of dressy flats and come-hither pumps for the demure shoe freak. *297–299 Brompton Rd.* ☎ *0207/584-9178. www.lkbennett. com. AE, DC, MC, V. Tube: S. Kensington. Map p 73.*

★★ **Mimi** CHELSEA This little boutique carries clothes and accessories from trendsetters Anya Hindmarch, Rock & Republic, Nanette Lepore, True Religion, and others. *309 King's Rd.* ☎ *0207/349-9699. www.mimilondon.co.uk. AE, DC, MC, V. Tube: Sloane Sq., then bus no. 11. Map p 73.*

★★ **The Natural Shoe Store** COVENT GARDEN Come here for the best of Birkenstock, Ecco, Arche, and other comfortable hippie styles now totally in vogue. *21 Neal St.* ☎ *0207/836-5254. www.the naturalshoestore.com. AE, DC, MC, V. Tube: Covent Garden. Map p 74.*

It's overpriced, but Harrods is a London shopping institution.

★★★ **Pandora** KNIGHTSBRIDGE
A big, well-organized shop featuring lots of designer names, shoes, and accessories left on consignment by frightfully fashionable Knightsbridge clotheshorses. *16–22 Cheval Place.* ☎ *0207/589-5289. www.pandora dressagency.com. AE, MC, V. Tube: Knightsbridge. Map p 73.*

★★★ **Topshop** MARYLEBONE
An absolute must-go for the younger generation, but even older women find something to love in this mecca of street fashion at decent prices. The flagship shop on Oxford Circus is a madhouse, but has the most variety. *216 Oxford St.* ☎ *0207/636-7700. www.topshop. com. AE, MC, V. Tube: Oxford Circus Sq. Map p 74.*

★★ **Vestry** CHELSEA   Vestry offers good prices and sweet clothes—perhaps more for the young and pretty, though the accessories will fit anyone. *120 King's Rd.* ☎ *0207/225-1323. www.vestry online.com. AE, DC, MC, V. Tube: Sloan Sq. Map p 73.*

Department Stores
★ **Harrods** KNIGHTSBRIDGE
From its food halls to its home entertainment centers, Harrods is a London institution—as well as an overhyped and overpriced bore. *87–135 Brompton Rd.* ☎ *0207/ 730-1234. www.harrods.com. AE, DC, MC, V. Tube: Knightsbridge. Map p 73.*

★★★ **John Lewis** MARYLEBONE
This is *the* place to find homey necessities such as sewing notions, fabrics, and kitchenware. Londoners can't live without it. *278–306 Oxford St.* ☎ *0207/629-7711. www.john lewis.co.uk. AE, DC, MC, V. Tube: Oxford Circus. Map p 74.*

★★★ **Selfridges** MARYLEBONE
Inside and out, this grand old department store is the best in town. The food halls are great, as are the fashions; it even offers tattooing and piercing. *400 Oxford St.* ☎ *0870/837-7377. www.selfridges. com. AE, DC, MC, V. Tube: Marble Arch. Map p 74.*

Food & Chocolates
★★★ **The Chocolate Society**
PIMLICO   With its amazing variations on a theme of cocoa beans, this shop offers creatively killer chocolate for grown-up tastes. *36 Elizabeth St.* ☎ *0207/259-9222. www.chocolate.co.uk. MC, V. Tube: Victoria or Sloane Sq. Map p 74.*

★★ Fortnum & Mason MAYFAIR

The city's ultimate grocer features goodies fit for the queen—or friends back home—plus gourmet picnic fare and specialty teas. *181 Piccadilly.* ☎ *0207/734-8040. www. fortnumandmason.co.uk. AE, DC, MC, V. Tube: Green Park. Map p 74.*

★ Harrods Food Halls KNIGHTS-

BRIDGE   Harrods sells loads of edible gifts branded with its famous name; be sure to ogle the remarkable ceilings in the produce and meat sections. *87–135 Brompton Rd.* ☎ *0207/730-1234. www.harrods. com. AE, DC, MC, V. Tube: Knightsbridge. Map p 73.*

★★ L'Artisan du Chocolat

CHELSEA   This award-winning shop makes quirky and delicious flavored chocolates and truffles for the connoisseur. Try the lavender chocolate—close your eyes, and you'll be in Provence. *89 Lower Sloane St.* ☎ *0207/824-8365. www.artisan duchocolat.com. MC, V. Tube: Sloane Sq. Map p 73.*

★★★ Ottolenghi KENSINGTON

This small shop is filled with exquisite European desserts—English puddings, French gâteaux, Italian *tortas*, German *bundts*—in every form and flavor. *Holland St.* ☎ *0207/937-0003. www.ottolenghi.co.uk. MC, V. Tube: Kensington High St. Map p 74.*

The ultimate London grocer, Fortnum & Mason can furnish a feast fit for a queen.

★★ Rococo Chocolate

CHELSEA   Chocoholics should head to this fine store, which stocks wittily shaped, high-cocoa-content confections and unique flavors (Earl Grey, rose, and more). *321 King's Rd.* ☎ *0207/352-5857. www.rococochocolates.com. MC, V. Tube: Sloan Sq., then bus no. 11. Map p 73.*

★★ Villandry MARYLEBONE

Hearty foodstuffs are displayed in a pleasing setting at this store, which also has a cafe and a restaurant. *170 Great Portland St.* ☎ *0207/631-3131. www.villandry.com. AE, DC, MC, V. Tube: Great Portland St. Map p 74.*

Home Decor

★★ Cologne & Cotton MARYLE-

BONE   Stock up here on elegant bed clothes of pure linen, and cotton sheets in soothing colors and simple designs. The pillowcases are gorgeous, and come in all sizes. *488 Marylebone High St.* ☎ *0207/ 486-0595. www.cologneandcotton. com. AE, MC, V. Tube: Baker St. Map p 74.*

★★ The Conran Shop SOUTH

KENSINGTON   Your best bets among the large and varied selection of high-priced merchandise here are the kitchenware and bath items. *Michelin House, 81 Fulham Rd.* ☎ *0207/589-7401. www. conran.com. AE, MC, V. Tube: S. Kensington. Map p 73.*

★★★ The General Trading

Company CHELSEA   Started in the 1920s, this shop sells useful as well as merely charming household goods and clever knickknacks from all over the world. *2 Symons St.* ☎ *0207/730-0411. www. general-trading.co.uk. AE, MC, V. Tube: Sloane Sq. Map p 73.*

★ Graham & Green NOTTING

HILL   Lighting, stationery, and attractive home-decor whatnots fill

Knowledgeable dealers and high-quality antiques are the hallmark of Bermondsey Market.

Graham & Green's two shops, located across the street from one another. *4 & 10 Elgin Crescent. ☎ 0207/727-4594. www.graham andgreen.co.uk. AE, MC, V. Tube: Notting Hill. Map p 74.*

★★ **India Jane** CHELSEA This store culls the best of India's most dignified furnishings and decor, and sells well-priced knickknacks and bibelots. *140 Sloane St. ☎ 0207/ 730-1070. www.indiajane.co.uk. AE, MC, V. Tube: Sloane Sq. Map p 73.*

★★★ **Summerill & Bishop** HOLLAND PARK Shop here for a sumptuous collection of French housewares, from efficient, humble radiator dusters to the finest table settings and cookery. *100 Portland St. ☎ 0207/221-4566. www.summerill andbishop.com. AE, MC, V. Tube: Holland Park. Map p 74.*

Jewelry
★ **Boodle & Dunthorne** KNIGHTSBRIDGE One of England's oldest jewelers (opened in 1798), B&D has resident designers who keep its collection fresh and

modern. *1 Sloane St. ☎ 0207/235-0111. AE, DC, MC, V. Tube: Knightsbridge. Map p 73.*

★ **Butler & Wilson** SOUTH KENS-INGTON You won't have to remort-gage your house to buy this store's beautiful costume and silver jewelry. It's *the* best shop in town for tiaras. *189 Fulham Rd. ☎ 0207/352-8255. www.butlerandwilson.co.uk. AE, MC, V. Tube: S. Kensington. Map p 73.*

★★ **Hirst Antiques** NOTTING HILL Something of a jewelry museum. You'll find extravagant vintage cos-tume baubles from European cat-walks of yore, and some interesting new gems as well. *59 Pembridge Rd. ☎ 0207/727-9364. www.hirst antiques.co.uk. MC, V. Tube: Notting Hill Gate. Map p 74.*

★★★ **Ritz Fine Jewelry** ST. JAMES Arguably the best hotel jewelry shop in the world, thanks to its collections of well-set semi-precious gems and serious rocks. Of course, when the hotel is the Ritz, it had better be the best. *150 Piccadilly. ☎ 0207/409-1312. www.ritzfinejewellery.com. AE, MC, V. Tube: Green Park. Map p 74.*

Lingerie
★★ **Agent Provocateur** SOHO Provocative, indeed! This store's sexy underclothes are works of art. If you've fallen off your diet, don't bother walking inside. *6 Broadwick St. ☎ 0207/439-0229. www.agent provocateur.com. AE, DC, MC, V. Tube: Piccadilly. Map p 74.*

★★ **La Senza** FITZROVIA Come here for classy, well-priced lingerie; some of the bras are almost too beautiful to hide beneath clothing. *162 Oxford St. ☎ 0207/580-3559. www.lasenza.com. AE, DC, MC, V. Tube: Oxford Circus. Map p 74.*

★ **Marks & Spencer** MARYLE-BONE This beloved, reliable outlet for comfy cotton underwear for men and women has kept up with the times, and offers a lot more than old-lady knickers. *458 Oxford St.* ☎ *0207/935-7954. www.marksand spencer.com. AE, DC, MC, V. Tube: Marble Arch. Map p 74.*

★ **Rigby & Peller** KNIGHTS-BRIDGE The corsetiere to the queen specializes in classy underwear, bathing suits (ask for "swimming costumes"), and finely engineered brassieres. *2 Hans Rd.* ☎ *0207/589-9293. www.rigbyand peller.com. AE, DC, MC, V. Tube: Knightsbridge. Map p 73.*

Markets

★ **Bermondsey (New Caledonian) Market** BERMONDSEY If you're up at 4am on a Friday, join the crush of dealers fighting over the estate goods and antiques sold here. Stalls are pretty much all packed up and gone by 9am. *Corner of Bermondsey St. & Long Lane.* ☎ *0207/969-1500. Some dealers take credit cards. Tube: Bermondsey. Map p 75.*

★★★ **Portobello Road Market** NOTTING HILL Saturday is the best day to join the throngs at Portobello's famous antiques market, although you can do some weekday shopping as well. Bring cash. *Portobello Rd. (from Notting Hill end to Ladbroke Grove). Some dealers take credit cards. www.portobelloroad. co.uk. Tube: Notting Hill. Map p 74.*

★★ **Spitalfields Market** SHOREDITCH Head to Spitalfields' huge, newly renovated market on Sunday for organic produce, ethnic clothes, knickknacks, and handmade crafts. *Commercial St.* ☎ *0207/247-8556. Most dealers take cash only. www. visitspitalfields.com. Tube: Liverpool St. Map p 75.*

Museum Shops

★ kids **British Museum** BLOOMSBURY The B.M. sells inexpensive key chains, children's toys, fine reproductions, gorgeous scarves, and great T-shirts themed to its collections. *Great Russell St.* ☎ *0207/636-1555. www.thebritish museum.ac.uk. AE, DC, MC, V. Tube: Russell Sq. Map p 74.*

★★ **National Gallery Gift Shop** WEST END The city's best source for art-related books and stationery, this shop also sells excellent calendars, cool T-shirts, and lots of artsy gifts. *Trafalgar Sq.* ☎ *0207/747-2885. www.nationalgallery.org.uk. AE, DC, MC, V. Tube: Charing Cross. Map p 74.*

★★★ kids **Victoria and Albert Museum** SOUTH KENSINGTON This must-stop shop sells everything from postcards to jewelry. Cool finds include hand-painted tools and nostalgic toys. *Cromwell Rd.* ☎ *0207/942-2000. www.vam.ac.uk. AE, DC, MC, V. Tube: S. Kensington. Map p 73.*

The National Gallery sells prints of its masterpieces, including Jan Van Eyck's Arnolfini Marriage.

The Best Shopping

Toys

★ kids Hamley's PICCADILLY
London's answer to FAO Schwarz
sports seven floors of fun and
games. There's a kid-thrilling selection of more than 35,000 toys and
games. *189–196 Regent St.* ☎ *0870/
333-2455. www.hamleys.com. AE,
DC, MC, V. Tube: Piccadilly Circus.
Map p 74.*

★ kids Harrods Toy World
KNIGHTSBRIDGE   There is something here for all ages, plus kiddie-
size cars and life-size stuffed
animals. Be prepared for a bad
case of the "gimmes" from your
kids. *4th Floor, 87–135 Brompton Rd.*
☎ *0207/730-1234. www.harrods.
com. AE, DC, MC, V. Tube: Knightsbridge. Map p 73.*

★★★ kids Honey Jam NOTTING
HILL   Created by two mums, this
fabulously fun and on-target toy
shop sells fine toys from Europe and
crazy little gimcracks for party bags.
There's also a small selection of
adorable clothes. *267 Portobello Rd.*
☎ *0207/243-0449. www.honeyjam.
co.uk. MC, V. Tube: Ladbroke Grove.
Map p 74.*

**★★★ kids The Print Gallery
Art Shop** KENSINGTON   For creative kids and grown-ups, this is one
of the most crammed-full arts and

*Selfridges is the best department store in
London. See p 80.*

crafts shops in London and is
sourced from all over Europe. Stock
up on craft kits and materials for
rainy afternoons. *22 Pembridge Rd.*
☎ *0207/221-8885. AE, DC, MC, V.
Tube: Notting Hill Gate. Map p 74.*

Woolens

★★ Pringle of Scotland
CHELSEA   Putting its rep for corn-
ball golf cardigans behind it, this
luxury retailer now sells an assortment of dressy casual-wear and
woolens that are very much up to
the minute. *141 Sloane St.* ☎ *0207/
259-1660. www.pringle-of-scotland.
co.uk. AE, DC, MC, V. Tube: Sloane
Sq. Map p 73.* ●

Hamley's vast toy selection makes it a family favorite.

6 The Great Outdoors

Hyde Park

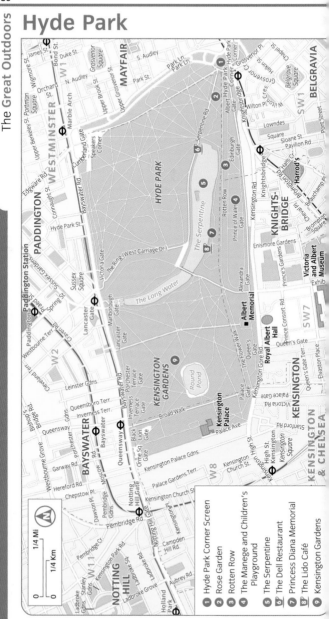

1 Hyde Park Corner Screen
2 Rose Garden
3 Rotten Row
4 The Manege and Children's Playground
5 The Serpentine
6/7 The Dell Restaurant
7 Princess Diana Memorial
8/7 The Lido Café
9 Kensington Gardens

Previous page: Hyde Park is one of the best places in London to go for outdoor recreation

Since 1536, when Henry VIII appropriated the land from the monks of Westminster Abbey for hunting, 142-hectare (351-acre) Hyde Park has been the scene of duels, highway robbery, and sport. Today, this Royal Park, the site of London's Great Exhibition of 1851, is a beloved oasis of green in the midst of the city, a great place for horseback riding in London, and the best seat in town for viewing Londoners at play. START: **Hyde Park Corner Tube Station**

1 ★★ **Hyde Park Corner Screen.** Erected in 1828, this imposing park entrance (one of six park entryways) was designed by Decimus Burton, the noted architect responsible for much of Hyde Park's layout. The triple-arched screen is composed of Ionic columns, bronzed ironwork, and carved friezes inspired by the Elgin Marbles (p 31, **3**). Unfortunately, it's being degraded by air pollution at this busy traffic circle. ⏱ *10 min.*

2 ★★ kids **Rose Garden.** From the Rose Garden, a riot of color in the early summer, you can admire the back of Apsley House (p 21, **2**) and Wellington Arch's majestic statue, *Winged Victory* (erected to commemorate the Duke of Wellington's war triumphs), in the east. The garden is filled with fountains and climbing rose trellises, both much loved by kids. Its central fountain is ringed with benches where you can sit with a picnic lunch, as hopeful (and picturesque) sparrows flutter around. ⏱ *20–30 min.*

3 ★★ kids **Rotten Row.** In the late 1680s, William III ordered 300 lamps to be hung from trees along this 2.4km (1.5-mile) riding path—whose name is an English corruption of its original appellation, *Route de Roi* ("King's Road")—in a vain attempt to stop the plague of high-waymen active in the park. Nowadays, it's where horses carrying riders through the park often decide it's time to canter, possibly sensing the echoes of the wild and dangerous carriage races that took place here over a century ago. If you want to give it a try, the best horses in the park are at the **Ross Nye Stables,** 8 Bathurst Mews (☎ 0207/262-3791). ⏱ *1 hr. On the southern boundary of the park. 1-hr. rides start at £40.*

Many Londoners retreat to Hyde Park for peace and quiet.

④ ★★★ kids The Manege and Children's Playground. At the Manege, a special riding arena for royal steeds, you may be lucky enough to see all the queen's men exercising all the queen's horses or practicing for a ceremonial event. The adjacent playground has all the equipment a kid might want, plus a nice view of the riding ring. 🕐 *15 min. Off S. Carriage Dr.*

⑤ ★★★ kids The Serpentine. Queen Caroline had the Westbourne River dammed in 1730 to create the Serpentine Lake, upon which she moored two royal yachts. This lovely lake is now the premiere boating spot in London for the masses. Should you venture out on the water, your yacht will be a tad less splendid than the queen's— you can choose from among 110 paddle boats and rowboats at the Boat House. If you want to sit out an adventure on the high seas, you can entertain yourself watching the in-line skaters who love this stretch of the park. 🕐 *1 hr. Blue-bird Boats Ltd., Serpentine Rd.* ☎ *0207/262-1330. Hourly rentals £6 adults, £2.50 kids, £15 family. Mar–Oct 10am–5pm.*

⑥ ★★ kids The Dell Restaurant has the best view of the Serpentine in the park, and serves hot meals, sandwiches, and drinks (wine included) that are a cut above the usual park cafeteria cuisine. You're welcome to picnic on the tables outside. *Eastern side of the Serpentine.* ☎ *0207/706-0464. $.*

⑦ ★ kids Princess Diana Memorial. This contemporary granite fountain, across the Serpentine from the Boat House,

Hyde Park's Serpentine is London's best spot for boating.

was opened by the queen in July 2004. No less dogged by controversy than the woman who inspired it, the 700-ton, £6.5-million fountain has suffered from flooding, closures and a slippery bottom. Children, who were meant to splash around happily in its cascading waters, are now restricted to toe-dipping by the omnipresent security guards. 🕐 *20 min. Near the Lido, south of the Serpentine.*

⑧ ★ kids The Lido Café offers blah food but is a good spot for a bathroom break, a cuppa, and good views. Sitting on the outdoor terrace, you may see people swimming in the adjacent Lido Pool, unfazed by the geese droppings. *South side of the Serpentine Terrace.* ☎ *0207/706-7098. $.*

⑨ ★★★ kids Kensington Gardens. Originally a part of Hyde Park, the 111-hectare (274-acre) Kensington Gardens were

Kensington Garden's famous statue of Peter Pan (p 89).

partitioned into an exclusive pre-serve of royalty in the 18th century, and were opened to the public only in the early 1800s. Originally laid out in Dutch style (emphasizing water, avenues, and topiaries), the attractive gardens are especially popular with families.

ensington Gardens Highlights

The bronze **9A** ★★ kids **Peter Pan Statue** was sculpted in 1912 by Sir George Frampton at the behest of author J. M. Barrie and is the most visited landmark in the park. A short walk north and you'll arrive at **9B** ★★★ kids **The Italian Gardens,** which echoed the rage for all things Italian when it was built in 1861. Generations of children have plied model boats at the **9C** ★★★ kids **Round Pond,** built in 1728. Today you'll also find adults trying out more sophisticated models. West of the pond is the **9D Broad Walk.** Nineteenth-century ladies and gentlemen promenaded along this tree-lined path past Kensington Palace, and flirted by the nearby bandstand. Peek through the front gates of Kensington Palace at the **9E** ★★★ kids **Sunken Gardens,** which were planted in 1909 and inspired by the Tudor gardens at Hampton Court Palace. End your tour at the exquisite **9F** ★★★ kids **Orangery Café,** where a very good tea is offered, and the atmosphere is airy and refined. ⏱ *2–3 hr. Go in the afternoon.* ☎ *0203/166-6112. www.hrp. org.uk. Tube: Kensington High St., Queensway, or Lancaster Gate. $$.*

Regent's Park

1 Grand Union Canal
2 Winfield House
3 London Zoo
4 The Honest Sausage
5 Bandstand and Open Air Theater
6 Queen Mary's Gardens
7 Queen Mary's Garden Café
8 Boating Lake

This 197-hectare (487-acre) gem started out as a hunting ground for Henry VIII, who liked to gallop here from Whitehall for the exercise. The park's ambitious design by John Nash (1752–1835) followed the romantic ideal of *rus in urbe* (country in the city), but what I love best about it is the carefully created sophistication of its many flower beds, its formal gardens with fountains, and the ornamental lake with its bridge and rowboats. It's more *urbe* than *rus* with its civilized decorative features and activities, and the leafy paths are lined with benches good for conversations, sunning, or people-watching. START: **Camden Town Station**

① ★★ kids **Grand Union Canal.** Londoners once traveled the city by boat when Regent's Park was in its infancy, and this is your chance to follow in their wake. The Grand Union Canal, opened in 1814, now covers 220km (137 miles) of waterways connecting the river Thames and the Chiltern Hills in Oxfordshire. Water buses now ply the scenic Regent's Canal section (opened in 1820) and will take you from Camden Lock's markets through the neighborhoods of colorful houseboats and grand Victorian houses on either side of the canal path in Little Venice—an area whose name is more wishful than accurate (there's just the one canal). Your final destination is the London Zoo inside Regent's Park, for which you can buy slightly discounted combo tickets before getting on the boat. ⏱ *50 min. Camden Lock.* ☎ *0207/482-2660. www.london waterbus.com. One-way tickets £6 adults, £4.30 kids 3–15. Year-round, depending on the weather.*

② **Winfield House.** As you sail, notice to your left the 4.6m (15-ft.) gates protecting a fine mansion beyond. Woolworth heiress Barbara Hutton built this Georgian mansion in 1936, adding extensive gardens and trees. A year after World War II, Hutton donated the antiques-filled home to the American government for use as the official residence of the U.S. ambassador. Unfortunately, you have to be an invited guest to enter.

Boats line the Grand Union Canal in Regent's Park.

3 ★★★ kids **London Zoo.** When this former zoology center opened to the public in 1847, many of its captives, such as Jumbo the Elephant (later bought by P. T. Barnum and shipped off to the U.S.), were celebrities. Visitors who complain about the high price of admission might feel differently about this venerable institution if they know that roughly one-sixth of its 650 species (about 5,000 animals reside here) are endangered—and that the zoo's world-renowned breeding program is the only thing preventing their extinction. I'm particularly fond of the reptile house, and the gorillas and other simians. ⏱ *2 hr.; longer for families. Outer Circle, Regent's Park.* ☎ *0207/722-3333. www.zsl.org. £17 adults, £16 seniors, £14 kids 3–15, £56 family. Daily 10am–5:30pm.*

If the smell of frying onions at **4** ★★ **The Honest Sausage** doesn't whet your appetite, nothing will. The menu features organic and relatively healthy lunch options. Best of all, there's a covered veranda to shelter you from sun and rain. *Broadwalk, Regent's Park.* ☎ *0207/224-3872. www.honest sausage.com. $.*

5 **Bandstand and Open Air Theater.** From late May to early September, these two stages feature alfresco concerts and plays, most notably Shakespearean comedies staged by the English Shakespeare Company. *See p 135.*

6 ★★★ kids **Queen Mary's Gardens.** Laid out in the 1930s, these regal gardens lie at the heart of the park's Inner Circle and are a place of enchanting colors, fragrances, and watery vistas. The fabulous and carefully tended Rose Gardens are especially beautiful in spring. ⏱ *30 min. Inner Circle.*

Food kiosks scattered around Regent's Park offer sandwiches and drinks. A less informal option is **7** ★★ **Queen Mary's Garden Café,** which sells a good variety of salads and sandwiches, as well as wine and beer, that you can enjoy on a lovely terrace. *Queen Mary's Garden, adjacent to Rose Garden.* ☎ *0207/935-5729. $.*

8 ★★ kids **Boating Lake.** Operating on a schedule that changes with the weather, Park Boats rents paddle boats and rowboats you can take out on this picturesque lake. Though the concession is usually closed midweek and in winter, you may be able to go boating on any sunny warm day, whatever the season—be sure to call ahead. ⏱ *1 hr.* ☎ *0207/724-4069. Open weekends Mar–Nov 11am–6pm. Hourly rentals £6.50 adults, £4.40 kids, £20 family.* ●

A lioness watches snow fall on the Regent's Park Zoo.

The **Best Dining**

Dining Best Bets

Best for Keeping Kids Happy
★ Rainforest Café $$ 20–24 Shaftsbury Ave. (p 106)

Best Vegetarian
★★★ Eat And Two Veg $$ 50 Marylebone High St. (p 101)

Best Place for Beef
★★★ Gaucho Grill $$ 19 Swallow St. (p 101)

Best Self-Service or Take-away
★★ Whole Foods Market Dining Halls $ 63–97 Kensington High St. (p 108)

Best Neighborhood Italian
★★★ The Ark $$ 122 Palace Gardens Terrace (p 100)

Best Afternoon Tea
★★★ Goring Hotel $$$ Beeston Place (p 102)

Best In-Store Cafe
★★★ 202 (Nicole Farhi) $$ 202 Westbourne Grove (p 107)

Best Cheap Eats
★ Café in the Crypt $ St. Martin-in-the-Fields, Duncannon St. (p 101)

Best American Noshes
★★★ Automat American Brasserie $$$ 33 Dover St. (p 100)

Best Fish and Chips
★★★ Geale's $$ 2 Farmer St. (p 102)

Most Interesting Interior
★★★ Toto's $$$ Walton House, Walton St. (p 107)

Best Olde England Vibe
★★ Rules $$ 35 Maiden Lane (p 106)

Best View
★★ Oxo Tower Brasserie $$$ Oxo Tower Wharf, Bargehouse St. (p 104)

Previous page: One of the tastiest ways to experience London is a traditional afternoon tea.

Best Stargazing
★★★ The Wolseley $$$ 160 Piccadilly (p 108)

Best Extravagant
★★★ Gordon Ramsay $$$$$ 68 Royal Hospital Rd. (p 102)

Most Demented Decor
★★★ Sketch $$$ 9 Conduit St. (p 107)

Best Thai
★★★ Nahm $$$ Halkin Hotel, Halkin St. (p 104)

Best French
★★★ Le Gavroche $$$$$ 43 Upper Brook St. (p 103)

Best Greek
★★★ Halepi $$ 18 Leinster Terrace (p 102)

Best Indian
★★ Tamarind $$$ 20 Queen St. (p 107)

Most Romantic
★★★ Lindsay House $$$$ 21 Romilly St. (p 103)

For traditional British cuisine, you can't do much better than Rules.

Notting Hill Dining

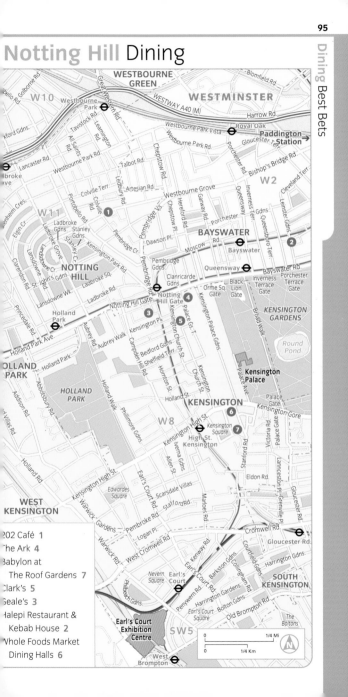

Kensington Dining

Bedford Gdns.

Sheffield Terr.

Kensington Palace

KENSINGTON GARDENS

Round Pond

Hornton St.

Campden Hill Rd.

Holland St.

Kensington Church St.

Palace Ave.

Broad Walk

Palace Gate

The Flower Walk

Alb Memo

Queen's Gate

Kensington Rd.

Kensington C

W8

High St. Kensington

Victoria Rd.

Palace Gate

Kensington Rd.

Royal Albert Hall

Holland Walk

Phillimore Gdns.

Kensington Square

Queen's Gate

Prin

HOLLAND PARK

Kensington High St.

Iverna Gdns.

Allen St.

KENSINGTON

Queen's Gate Terr.

Eldon Rd.

Elvaston Place

Earl's Court Rd.

Scarsdale Villas

Stafford Rd.

Marloes Rd.

Stamford Rd.

Launceston Pl.

Grenville Pl.

Gloucester Rd.

Queen's Gate Pl.

Edwardes Square

Pembroke Rd.

Logan Pl.

Cromwell Rd.

Cromwell Rd.

Gloucester Rd.

Courtfield Gdns.

2

West Cromwell Rd.

Collingham Rd.

Harrington Gdns.

Harringt

Phillbeach Gdns.

Nevern Square

Kenway Rd.

Earl's Court Rd.

Barkston Gdns.

SOUTH KENSINGTON

Gloucester Rd.

Bina Gdns.

Old Brompt

Warwick Rd.

Trebovir Rd.

Penywern Rd.

Earl's Court

Harrington Gardens

Bolton Gdns.

The Little Boltons

The Boltons

Roland Gardens

Drayton Gardens

Earl's Court Exhibition Centre

SW5

Old Brompton Rd.

EARL'S COURT

3

Redcliffe Gardens

Tregunter Rd.

Hollywood Rd.

Gilston Rd.

4

Gardens

Be

Earl's Court Square

Finborough Road

West Brompton

Seagrave Rd.

BROMPTON CEMETERY

SW10

Park W

Limerston St.

Lillie Rd.

Ongar Rd.

WEST BROMPTON

Fulham Road

Edith Grove

HAMMERSMITH

Fulham Broadway

Stamford Bridge Stadium (Chelsea Football Club)

SW6

Fulham Road

King's Rd.

| 0 | | 1/4 Mi |
| 0 | | 1/4 Km |

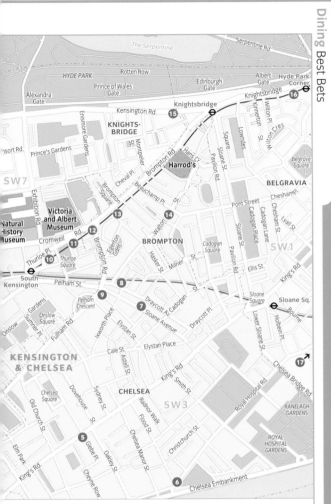

Balans **3**
Bibendum **9**
Brasserie St. Quentin **12**
Café Creperie of Hampstead **10**
The Good Earth **13**
Gordon Ramsay **6**
Itsu **8**
Kensington Place **1**
Mr. Chow's **15**

La Poule au Pot **17**
My Old Dutch
  Pancake House **5**
Orsini's Cafe **11**
Paul **2**
Toto's **14**
Pizza on the Park **16**
Poissonnerie de l'avenue **7**
Vingt Quatre **4**

West End Dining

Automat American	Lindsay House 21	Rainforest Café 22
Brasserie 15	Maroush V 4	The Ritz Palm Court 13
Café In the Crypt 26	Mildred's 18	Roast 32
Eat and Two Veg Diner 1	Momo 17	Royal China Club 3
Fahrkreldine 11	Nahm 8	Rules 30
Food for Thought 28	Nobu 7	Shogun 6
Gaucho Grill 24	Oxo Tower Brasserie 31	Sketch 16
The Gay Hussar 20	Porters English	Tamarind 10
The Goring 9	Restaurant 29	Texas Embassy Cantina 25
The Ivy 23	The Portrait 27	Wagamama 19
angan's Brasserie 12	The Providores	The Wolseley Café
e Gavroche 5	and Tapa Room 2	Restaurant 14

London Restaurants A to Z

★★★ **The Ark** KENSINGTON *ITALIAN* A modest building houses one of the best Italian restaurants in London. Everything is made on the premises, from the fresh pasta to the tiramisu, which is an experience in itself. *122 Palace Gardens Terrace.* ☎ *0207/ 229-4024. www.ark-restaurant.com. Entrees £13–£20. AE, MC, V. Tube: Notting Hill Gate. Map p 95.*

★★★ kids **Automat American Brasserie** MAYFAIR *AMERICAN* This elegantly appointed re-creation of a classic diner offers good old Yankee meals for the well-heeled Londoner, and is a little piece of the U.S.A. for homesick visitors. *33 Dover St.* ☎ *0207/499-3033. www.automat-london.com. Entrees £7–£20. AE, DC, MC, V. Breakfast, lunch & dinner daily. Tube: Green Park. Map p 98.*

★★ **Babylon at The Roof Gardens** KENSINGTON *MODERN EURO-PEAN* Come here on a sunny day to admire the wondrous view, and take advantage of the set lunch prices. *99 Kensington High St. (entrance on Derry St.).* ☎ *0207/937-7994. www. roofgardens.com. Entrees £16–£25. AE, DC, MC, V. Lunch & dinner daily. Tube: Kensington High St. Map p 95.*

★★ kids **Balans** EARLS COURT *MODERN BRITISH* The reasonably priced and varied menu make this an old reliable for breakfast, lunch, and dinner. *249 Old Brompton Rd.* ☎ *0207/244-8838. www.balans.co.uk. Entrees £8–£15. AE, DC, MC, V. Breakfast, lunch & dinner daily. Tube: Earl's Court. Map p 96.*

★★ **Bibendum** SOUTH KENSING-TON *MODERN EUROPEAN* Reliably good food, with an emphasis on fresh fish, and an airy location in the stylish Art Nouveau Michelin Building make this restaurant an old favorite. *81 Fulham Rd.* ☎ *0207/ 581-5817. www.bibendum.co.uk. Entrees £20–£30. AE, DC, MC, V. Lunch & dinner daily. Tube: S. Kensington. Map p 97.*

★★★ **Brasserie St. Quentin** KNIGHTSBRIDGE *CLASSIC FRENCH* This classy, friendly Paris-style brasserie shines with simple but

Bibendum and its oyster bar serve up some of London's freshest seafood.

delicious cuisine. *243 Brompton Rd.* ☎ *0207/589-8005. Entrees £13–£25. AE, DC, MC, V. Lunch & dinner daily. Tube: Knightsbridge. Map p 97.*

★ **kids Café Creperie of Hampstead** SOUTH KENSINGTON *FRENCH* Treat yourself to one of this authentic French creperie's many savory galettes and sweet crepes. *2 Exhibition Rd.* ☎ *0207/589-8947. Entrees £6–£10. MC, V. Lunch & dinner daily. Tube: S. Kensington. Map p 97.*

★ **kids Café In the Crypt** SOHO *BRITISH DINER* This award-winning cafeteria offers cheap and hearty meals, as well as a jolly good tea. *St. Martin-in-the-Fields, enter on Duncannon St.* ☎ *0207/766-1129. www2.stmartin-in-the-fields.org. Entrees £3–£10. MC, V. Lunch & dinner daily. Tube: Charing Cross. Map p 98.*

★★★ **Clark's** KENSINGTON *MODERN EUROPEAN* Chef Sally Clark gratifies taste buds in her charming dining room, using only the freshest ingredients in her excellent, ever-changing dishes. *122 Kensington Church St.* ☎ *0207/221-9225. www.sallyclark.com. Entrees £16–£20. AE, DC, MC, V. Lunch & dinner daily. Tube: Notting Hill Gate. Map p 95.*

★★★ **kids Eat and Two Veg Diner** MARYLEBONE *VEGETARIAN* With its big booths and extensive menu, this is a classic American diner for noncarnivores. All the hearty classics—burgers, stews, and roasts—have been adapted for meat-free dining. *50 Marylebone High St.* ☎ *0207/258-8595. www. eatandtwoveg.com. Entrees £6–£15. MC, V. Breakfast, lunch & dinner daily. Tube: Baker St. Map p 98.*

★★★ **kids Fahkreldine** MAYFAIR *LEBANESE* London's best Lebanese restaurant, thanks to its traditional menu, solid service, and

You can't leave London without trying the city's famous fish and chips.

fine views of Green Park. *85 Piccadilly.* ☎ *0207/493-3424. www.fahkreldine. co.uk. Entrees £13–£20. AE, MC, V. Lunch & dinner daily; Sun brunch. Tube: Green Park. Map p 98.*

★★ **kids Food for Thought** COVENT GARDEN *VEGETARIAN* Since 1974, this tiny spot has been an underground favorite. The food is fresh, vegetarian, imaginative, and very healthy. *31 Neal St.* ☎ *0207/ 836-0239. Entrees £5–£8. No credit cards. Breakfast, lunch & dinner Mon–Sat; lunch Sun. Tube: Covent Garden. Map p 98.*

★★★ **kids Gaucho Grill** WEST END *ARGENTINEAN* The best Argentinean dining in Europe, with an emphasis on grilled beef. There's also a small selection of South American wines. *19 Swallow St.* ☎ *0207/734-4040. www.gaucho-grill.com. Entrees £10–£30. AE, DC, MC, V. Lunch & dinner daily. Tube: Piccadilly. Map p 98.*

★★ **The Gay Hussar** SOHO *HUNGARIAN* Since 1953, this tiny dining room has served tasty goulashes, potato pancakes, blini, and other comfort foods to locals and tourists. Try the wild cherry soup. *2 Greek St.* ☎ *0207/437-0973. www.gayhussar.co.uk. Entrees*

£10–£15. MC, V. Lunch & dinner daily. Tube: Tottenham Court. Map p 98.

★★★ **Geale's** KENSINGTON *FISH* Yes, it's got caviar, fresh flowers, linen table clothes, and other posh touches, but go for the humble fish and chips, among the best in London. The sticky toffee pudding is another classic done well at this popular restaurant. *2 Farmer St.* ☎ *0207/727-7528. Entrees £10–£13. AE, MC, V. Lunch & dinner daily. Tube: Notting Hill Gate. Map p 95.*

★★ **kids** **The Good Earth** KNIGHTSBRIDGE *CHINESE* More elegant than your usual Chinese restaurant, with prices to match, this Knightsbridge favorite does a great Beijing duck. It's good for vegetarians, too. *233 Brompton Rd.* ☎ *0207/584-3658. Entrees £10–£22. AE, MC, V. Lunch & dinner daily. Tube: Knightsbridge. Map p 97.*

★★★ **Gordon Ramsay** CHELSEA *FRENCH* Its three Michelin stars are no joke: This is serious haute cuisine at its best, and dedicated gastronomes find it worth every pound. *68 Royal Hospital Rd.* ☎ *0207/352-4441. www.gordonramsay.com. Set lunch £40, dinner £70. AE, DC, MC, V. Lunch & dinner Mon–Fri. Tube: Sloane Sq. Map p 97.*

★★★ **Goring Hotel** VICTORIA *BRITISH* Mutton broth, steak and kidney pie, grilled liver, fish galore, and crumble: You can't get more English than the menu at the Goring, a hotel whose dining room and garden recall Edwardian elegance at its finest. Afternoon tea is done just right. *Beeston Place.* ☎ *0207/396-9000. www.goringhotel.co.uk. Set lunch £33, dinner £44, afternoon tea £25. AE, DC, MC, V. Lunch & dinner daily. Tube: Victoria. Map p 98.*

★★★ **kids** **Halepi Restaurant & Kebab House** BAYSWATER *GREEK* Bring the whole family to share classic home-style Greek dishes and simple Mediterranean-grilled fish and meat. The baklava is the best around. *18 Leinster Terrace.* ☎ *0207/262-1070. www.halepi.co.uk. Entrees £10–£18. MC, V. Lunch & dinner daily. Tube: Bayswater. Map p 95.*

★★ **kids** **Itsu** SOUTH KENSINGTON *ASIAN* A fun place, where diners choose from an excellent selection of small but pricey dishes that roll by on a conveyor belt. *118 Draycott Ave.* ☎ *0207/590-2400. www.itsu.com. Entrees £5–£10. MC, V. Lunch & dinner daily. Tube: S. Kensington. Map p 97.*

★★ **The Ivy** COVENT GARDEN *MODERN BRITISH* The menu is

Some of the city's most innovative gourmet cuisine is found at Gordon Ramsay.

The Ivy's a great place for spotting celebrities.

surprisingly diverse (ranging from caviar to fish cakes to irresistible puddings) at this exclusive haunt of British celebs. For a fancy place, it's not terribly overpriced. *1 West St.* ☎ *0207/836-4751. www.the-ivy. co.uk. Entrees £12–£39. AE, DC, MC, V. Lunch & dinner daily. Tube: Leicester Sq. Map p 98.*

★★ **Kensington Place** KENSING-TON *MODERN BRITISH* Come here for innovative fresh fish dishes served in a modern, noisy dining room. *201 Kensington Church St.* ☎ *0207/727-3184. www.egami.co.uk. Entrees £16–£23. AE, DC, MC, V. Lunch & dinner daily. Tube: Notting Hill. Map p 96.*

★★ **La Poule au Pot** CHELSEA *FRENCH* This chic retro French bistro, much-loved by Londoners, brings a slice of rural France to Chelsea. The cozy atmosphere, friendly staff, and classic dishes always make eating here a joyous occasion. Ask for a large carafe of the house wine to complete the festive experience. *231 Ebury St.* ☎ *0207/730-7763. Entrees £15–£21. AE, MC, V. Lunch & dinner daily. Tube: Sloane Square. Map p 97.*

★★ kids **Langan's Brasserie** ST. JAMES *BRASSERIE* A big upscale brasserie with two noisy floors of dining, serving everything from spinach soufflé to fish and chips. *Stratton St.* ☎ *0207/491-8822. www.langansrestaurants.com. Entrees £14–£20. AE, DC, MC, V. Lunch & dinner Mon–Fri; dinner Sat. Tube: Green Park. Map p 98.*

★★★ **Le Gavroche** MAYFAIR *FRENCH* Internationally renowned chef Michel Roux oversees the kitchen at this Michelin three-star extravaganza serving classic French haute cuisine in a clubby, elegant dining room. *43 Upper Brook St.* ☎ *0207/408-0881. www.le-gavroche. co.uk. £48 prix-fixe lunch, £95 tasting menu. AE, DC, MC, V. Lunch & dinner Mon–Fri; dinner Sat. Tube: Marble Arch. Map p 98.*

★★★ **Lindsay House** SOHO *MODERN BRITISH* Richard Corrigan, one of London's most inventive chefs, uses French and Irish techniques to create English culinary wonders in a beautiful Regency dining room. *21 Romilly St.* ☎ *0207/439-0450. www.lindsayhouse.co.uk. Lunch entrees £12–£22; set dinner menu £56–£68. AE, DC, MC, V. Lunch & dinner Mon–Fri; dinner Sat. Tube: Piccadilly. Map p 98.*

★★ kids **Maroush V** MARYLEBONE *MIDDLE EASTERN* This branch of a popular London chain, known for its good value, offers a big menu that includes fresh-squeezed juices and excellent falafel. Open late. *4 Vere St.*

A sampling of the French haute cuisine served at the renowned Le Gavroche.

The Best Dining

☎ 0207/493-3030. www.maroush. com. Entrees £8–£15. AE, DC, MC, V. Breakfast, lunch & dinner daily. Tube: Bond St. Map p 98.

★★★ kids **Mildred's** SOHO *VEGE-TARIAN* The best vegetarian/vegan restaurant in London serves well-priced health food faves such as stir-fries, veggie burgers, salads, and juices. Don't skip the tasty desserts. *45 Lexington St.* ☎ *0207/494-1634. www.mildreds.co.uk. Entrees £7–£10. MC, V. Lunch & dinner daily. Tube: Piccadilly. Map p 98.*

★★★ **Mr. Chow's** KNIGHTSBRIDGE *CHINESE* The dining room demonstration of noodles being made each night is just one of the attractions at this perennially fashionable restaurant, the first of many Mr. Chow's in the world. Lovely service, excellent food, and not as pricey as you might fear. *151 Knightsbridge.* ☎ *0207/589-7347. www.mrchow.com. Entrees £12–£25. AE, DC, MC, V. Lunch & dinner daily. Tube: Knightsbridge. Map p 97.*

★★★ kids **Momo** MAYFAIR *MOR-ROCCAN* Decorated in Arabian Nights splendor, this West End success story is a wonderful place for a taste of exotic and fantastic *tagines* (Moroccan spiced stews)! *25 Heddon St.* ☎ *0207/434-4040. www.momo resto.com. Entrees £11–£18. AE, DC, MC, V. Lunch & dinner daily. Tube: Oxford Circus. Map p 98.*

★ kids **My Old Dutch Pancake House** CHELSEA *CREPERIE* Stick to the thin pancakes, which are as large as a pizza and topped with whatever you fancy. *221 King's Rd.* ☎ *0207/376-5650. www.myold dutch.com. Entrees £5–£8. AE, MC, V. Breakfast, lunch & dinner daily. Tube: Sloane Sq. Map p 97.*

★★★ **Nahm** BELGRAVIA *THAI* This chicly appointed Thai restaurant in the Halkin Hotel has been going strong for years, thanks to impeccable service and wizardry in the kitchen. A favorite among gourmands. *Halkin St.* ☎ *0207/333-1234. www.nahm.como.bz. Entrees £12–£18. AE, DC, MC, V. Lunch & dinner daily. Tube: Hyde Park Corner. Map p 98.*

★★★ **Nobu** MAYFAIR *JAPANESE/ FUSION* Famous for its glamour, its staggering tabs, and its creative sushi. *Metropolitan Hotel, 19 Old Park Lane.* ☎ *0207/376-5650. www.nobu restaurants.com. Entrees £15–£25. AE, MC, V. Lunch & dinner Mon–Fri; dinner Sat–Sun. Tube: Hyde Park Corner. Map p 98.*

★★★ kids **Orsini's Cafe** SOUTH KENSINGTON *ITALIAN* Opposite the V&A, this cafe right out of Naples features great daily specials, perfectly prepared pastas, and great cappuccino. *8a Thurloe Place.* ☎ *0207/581-5553. Entrees £7–£12. AE, MC, V. Breakfast, lunch & dinner daily. Tube: S. Kensington. Map p 97.*

★★ **Oxo Tower Brasserie** SOUTHBANK *GLOBAL FUSION* Get the best river views in London while dining on a somewhat pricey menu of dishes that combine Mediterranean, French, and Asian ingredients. The 1930s-style dining room is quite chic, but you should dine on the balcony in

Nobu's creative sushi attracts a glamorous crowd.

A traditional English breakfast.

summer. *Oxo Tower Wharf, Bargehouse St.* ☎ *0207/803-3888. www.harveynichols.com. Entrees £17–£34. AE, DC, MC, V. Lunch & dinner daily. Tube: Blackfriars. Map p 99.*

★★ **kids** **Paul** KENSINGTON *CAFE* Visit this popular branch of a Parisian cafe chain for its variety of bread, high-quality pastries, and excellent sandwiches on fresh baguettes. *73 Gloucester Rd.* ☎ *0207/373-1232. www.paul.fr. Entrees £3–£7. MC, V. Breakfast & lunch daily. Tube: Gloucester Rd. Map p 96.*

★★ **kids** **Pizza on the Park** KNIGHTSBRIDGE *PIZZA/ITALIAN* Live jazz makes this pizza joint more attractive than all its brethren in the city. *11–13 Knightsbridge.* ☎ *0207/235-5273. www.pizzaexpress.co.uk. Entrees £8–£15. AE, DC, MC, V. Breakfast, lunch & dinner daily. Tube: Hyde Park Corner. Map p 97.*

★★★ **Poissonnerie de l'Avenue** SOUTH KENSINGTON *FRENCH/SEAFOOD* A very old-school yet very friendly place, with impeccable service, excellent fish, creative French-influenced dishes, and desserts to die for. There's a great two-course set lunch for £20. *82 Sloane Ave.* ☎ *0207/589-2457. www.poissonneriedelavenue.com. Entrees £16–£30. AE, DC, MC, V. Lunch & dinner daily. Tube: S. Kensington. Map p 97.*

★ **kids** **Porters English Restaurant** COVENT GARDEN *TRADITIONAL BRITISH* The Earl of Bradford's eatery serves simple and traditional English food in the heart of Theaterland. The comfortable two-story restaurant is family-friendly, informal, and lively. Check the website for theater- or attractions-and-dinner deals. *17 Henrietta St.* ☎ *0207/836-6466. www.porters.uk.com. Entrees £10–£16. AE, MC, V. Lunch & dinner daily. Tube: Charing Cross. Map p 99.*

★ **The Portrait** SOHO *MODERN BRITISH* The big attraction here is the gorgeous view over Trafalgar Square, but the food—ranging from chargrilled Scottish sirloin to baked cod—is tasty, too. The excellent wine list features some organic vintages. *The National Portrait Gallery, St. Martin's Lane.* ☎ *0207/312-2490. www.searcys.co.uk. Entrees £12–£20. AE, DC, MC, V. Lunch daily; dinner Thurs–Fri. Tube: Charing Cross. Map p 98.*

★★ **kids** **The Providores and Tapa Room** MARYLEBONE *GLOBAL* The Tapa Room features savory breakfasts; head upstairs to the restaurant for interesting twists on global favorites. *109 Marylebone High St.* ☎ *0207/935-6175. www.theprovidores.co.uk. Entrees*

Head to Nahm for gourmet Thai in a chic setting.

£8–£17. AE, MC, V. Tapa Room: Breakfast, lunch & dinner daily. Restaurant: Lunch & dinner daily. Tube: Bond St. Map p 98.

★ kids **Rainforest Café** SOHO *AMERICAN* It's not a meal, it's a safari loaded with foliage and animatronic animals. Head to this kid-pleasing joint for the atmosphere, and stay for the coconut fried chicken. *20–24 Shaftsbury Ave.* ☎ *0207/434-3111. www.therain forestcafe.co.uk. Entrees £10–£16. AE, DC, MC, V. Lunch & dinner daily. Tube: Piccadilly. Map p 98.*

★★★ kids **The Ritz Palm Court** WEST END *ENGLISH TEA* Women, wear your best dress to this very deluxe (and pricey!) tea, served in a Versailles-like setting. Book way ahead. *150 Piccadilly.* ☎ *0207/493-8181. www.theritzhotel.co.uk. £37 per person. AE, DC, MC, V. Afternoon tea daily. Tube: Green Park. Map p 98.*

★★ kids **Roast** SOUTHWARK *BRITISH* Browse through trendy Borough market then retreat upstairs to this light restaurant with great views of St. Paul's. Dishes are classic British, made from locally sourced, seasonal produce; the contemporary decor adds a twist to the splendor of the historic market

architecture. *The Floral Hall, Borough Market, Stoney St.* ☎ *0207/940-1300. www.roast-restaurant. com. Entrees £12–£20. AE, MC, V. Breakfast, lunch & dinner daily. Tube: London Bridge. Map p 99.*

★★★ kids **Royal China Club** MARYLEBONE *CHINESE* Just a bit tonier than its sister restaurant down the street, this is the real deal for dim sum, with the kind of choice and quality you'd find in Hong Kong. *40–42 Baker St.* ☎ *0207/486-3898. www.royalchinaclub.com. Entrees £8–£38. AE, MC, V. Lunch & dinner daily. Tube: Baker St. Map p 98.*

★★ **Rules** COVENT GARDEN *TRADITIONAL ENGLISH* The most traditional Olde English restaurant in London, Rules dates back to 1798, and is a must for Anglophiles and lovers of roast beef and Yorkshire pudding. *35 Maiden Lane.* ☎ *0207 /836-5314. www.rules.co.uk. Entrees £10–£20. AE, MC, V. Lunch & dinner daily. Tube: Charing Cross. Map p 99.*

★★ **Shogun** MAYFAIR *JAPANESE* Enjoy sushi and other authentically prepared Japanese favorites in a dining room that resembles a medieval cellar—full of stone, wood, and atmosphere. *Adam's Row, beneath the Millennium May-*

A traditional high tea is served in an ultraluxe setting at the Ritz Palm Court.

The quirky Lecture Room at Sketch is a hot dining spot for London foodies.

air Hotel. ☎ 0207/493-1255.
Entrees £10–£25. AE, DC, MC, V.
Lunch & dinner daily. Tube: Bond St.
Map p 98.

★★★ Sketch MAYFAIR

FRENCH/MODERN BRITISH Sketch
is a must-see place, with its beyond-
quirky artful decor and its variety of
eating venues. The Lecture Room,
with Michelin-starred chef Pierre
Gagnaire, is where the serious gas-
tronomy goes on; but for less
money, go for tea at the Parlour or
lunch at the Glade. *9 Conduit St.*
☎ 0870/777-4488. www.sketch.
uk.com. Entrees £12–£100. AE, DC,
MC, V. Lunch & dinner daily. Tube:
Oxford Circus. Map p 98.

★★ Tamarind MAYFAIR INDIAN

Diners ranging from business execs
to couples appreciate this spot's elegant decor, and the imaginative
menu that goes beyond the usual
curries. *20 Queen St.* ☎ 0207/629-
3561. www.tamarindrestaurant.com.
Entrees £14–£22. AE, DC, MC, V.
Lunch & dinner daily. Tube: Green
Park. Map p 98.

★ kids Texas Embassy Cantina

SOHO TEX MEX Get knockout
margaritas and a Wild West atmosphere in a historic building that once
housed the owners of the *Titanic.*

1 Cockspur St. ☎ 0207/925-0077.
www.texasembassy.com. Entrees
£8–£15. AE, MC, V. Lunch & dinner
daily. Tube: Charing Cross. Map p 98.

★★★ kids Toto's KNIGHTSBRIDGE

ITALIAN Set in a beautiful old
building with a magnificent fireplace
and a foyer built around a big tree,
this is a great bet for an elegant cel-
ebration, perhaps enjoyed in its garden. *In Walton House, on Walton St.*
☎ 0207/589-0075. Entrees £12–£20.
AE, DC, MC, V. Lunch & dinner daily.
Tube: Knightsbridge. Map p 97.

★★★ kids 202 Café NOTTING

HILL BRITISHI What to do, eat or
shop? You can do both at this cafe
set in a Nicole Farhi shop, which is
probably why young mums love this
place, with its garden, great food,
friendly service . . . and the occasional sale on clothes and home
decor. *202 Westbourne Grove.*
☎ 0207/727-2722. www.nicole
farhi.com. Entrees £6–£14. AE, MC,
V. Breakfast & lunch daily. Tube:
Bayswater. Map p 95.

★ kids Vingt Quatre CHELSEA

DINER The best reason to come
to this busy diner is that it's always
open, serving blah brasserie food
to jet-lagged insomniacs and after-
hours clubbers. *325 Fulham Rd.*

Both the Moroccan cuisine and the exotic setting beckon diners to Momo.

☎ *0207/323-9223. www.vingt quatre.co.uk. Entrees £7–£15. MC, V. Open 24 hr. Tube: S. Kensington, then bus no. 14. Map p 96.*

★ **kids Wagamama** BLOOMS-BURY *JAPANESE*   You sit at large cafeteria-like tables where the noise level is considerable, but this popular Tokyo-style noodle chain is tops for reasonably priced Asian food. *4a Streatham St.* ☎ *0207/323-9223. www.wagamama.com. Entrees £6–£15. AE, MC, V. Lunch & dinner daily. Tube: Tottenham Court. Map p 98.*

★★ **kids Whole Foods Market Dining Halls** KENSINGTON *GLOBAL*   You'll love the wealth of options and reasonable prices at the top of the Whole Foods Market building. Excellent takeout and treats to bring back to your hotel room. *63–97 Kensington High St.* ☎ *0207/368-4500. www.wholefoods market.com. Entrees £4–£15. AE, MC, V. Breakfast, lunch & dinner daily. Tube: Kensington High St. Map p 95.*

★★★ **The Wolseley Café Restaurant** ST. JAMES *ENGLISH* This hugely popular restaurant on Piccadilly has a high-ceilinged Art Deco dining room, dishes out celeb sightings, and offers an extensive menu of decent value. And it serves breakfast! *160 Piccadilly.* ☎ *0207/499-6996. www.thewolseley.com. Entrees £10–£30. AE, DC, MC, V. Breakfast, lunch & dinner daily. Tube: Green Park. Map p 98.* ●

Wagamama is one of London's best options for well-priced Asian cuisine.

8

The Best **Nightlife**

Nightlife Best Bets

Best **Dance Club**
★★★ Fabric, *77a Charterhouse St.* (p 122)

Most **Diverse Entertainment**
★★★ Madame JoJo's, *8–10 Brewer St.* (p 122)

Best **Jazz Club**
★★★ Ronnie Scott's, *47 Frith St.* (p 123)

Most **Wacky Decor**
★ Beach Blanket Babylon, *45 Ledbury Rd.* (p 119)

Best **Club to Wear Your Bathing Suit To**
★★★ Aquarium, *256 Old St.* (p 121)

Most **Unpretentious**
★★★ Plastic People, *147–149 Curtain Rd.* (p 123)

Best **Name**
★★★ Mephisto, *254 Edgeware Rd.* (p 120)

Best **Views**
★★★ Vertigo 42, *25 Old Broad St.* (p 121)

Best **Historic Pub**
★★★ Ye Olde Cheshire Cheese, *145 Fleet St.* (p 125)

Ronnie Scott's, London's best jazz club

Best **for Blues**
★★ Ain't Nothin' But? The Blues Bar, *20 Kingly St.* (p 118)

Most **Elegant Pub/Bar**
★★★ The Audley, *41 Mount St.* (p 117)

Best **Place to Spot a Celeb**
★★★ The Social, *5 Little Portland St.* (p 123)

Best **Sports Bar**
★★ Sports Café, *80 Haymarket* (p 121)

Best **Gay Bar**
★★★ The Edge, *11 Soho Sq.* (p 119)

Best **Cocktail Lounge**
★★ Blue Bar, *Berkeley Hotel, Wilton Place* (p 119)

Best **Hotel Bar**
★★★ The Library, *Lanesborough Hotel, 1 Lanesborough Place* (p 120)

Best **Cocktails**
★★★ BBar, *43 Buckingham Palace Rd.* (p 119)

Most **Seductive**
★★★ Beduin Bar, *57–59 Charterhouse St., Smithfield* (p 119)

Most **Impressive Toilets**
★★★ Sketch, *9 Conduit St.* (p 123)

Best **People-Watching**
★ Chinawhite, *6 Air St.* (p 121)

Best **Overall Venue**
★★★ Proud Bar, *Stables Market, Chalk Farm Rd.* (p 120)

Previous page: Downing a pint of British ale at a London pub is a great way to experience the local nightlife.

Notting Hill Nightlife

each Blanket Babylon 1

oubadour Café 2

West End Nightlife

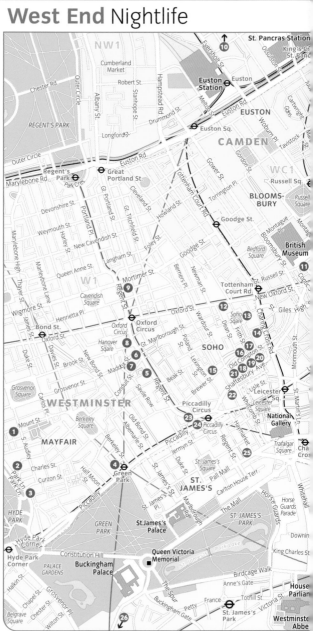

Admiral Duncan 16	The Edge 13	Opium 12
Ain't Nothin' But? The Blues Bar 5	Elysium Lounge 23	Paragon Lounge 8
	G-A-Y Bar 14	Proud Bar 10
The Audley 1	Green Carnation 18	The Rivoli Bar 4
Babushka 27		Ronnie Scott's 17
Bar Rumba 22	Guanabara 31	Sketch 6
BBar 26	Heaven 32	The Soho 19
Canal 125 28	The Lamb 29	Sports Café 25
Chinawhite 24	Madam JoJo's 15	The Social 9
Cittie of York 30	Museum Tavern 11	Waxy O'Connors 21
Coach & Horses 20		
Dorchester Bar 2	Noble Rot 7	Windows Bar 3

Kensington Nightlife

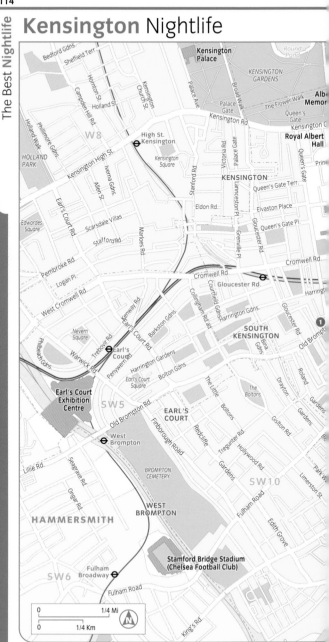

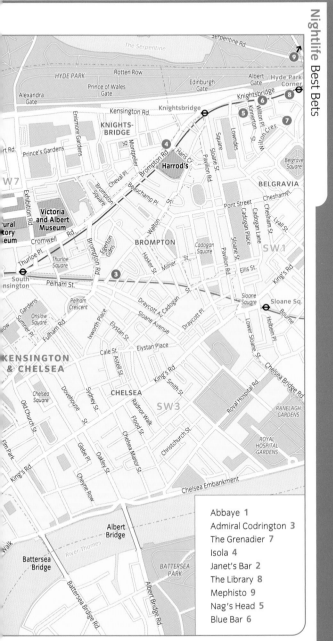

Abbaye 1
Admiral Codrington 3
The Grenadier 7
Isola 4
Janet's Bar 2
The Library 8
Mephisto 9
Nag's Head 5
Blue Bar 6

116

Nightlife in **The City**

93 Feet East 8
Aquarium 5
Beduin Bar 4
Fabric 3
Herbal 7
Ministry of Sound 10
Old Bank of England 1
Plastic People 6
Vertigo 42 11
Williamson's Tavern 9

London Nightlife A to Z

Pubs

★★ Admiral Codrington

CHELSEA   This pub has modern British cuisine, a friendly staff, a well-heeled crowd from neighboring Chelsea and South Kensington, and a nice atmosphere with a retractable glass roof. Outdoor tables handle overflow on warm evenings. *17 Mossup St.* ☎ *0207/581-0005. Tube: S. Kensington. Map p 115.*

★★ Admiral Duncan SOHO

This popular gay bar weathered a homophobe's bomb in 1999 and now offers bargain shots, cocktails, and a good selection of wines. Gay or straight, it's a mellow and friendly place to drink. *54 Old Compton St.* ☎ *0207/437-5300. Tube: Leicester Sq. Map p 112.*

★★★ The Audley MAYFAIR   This

is one of London's more beautiful old-school pubs, evocative of a Victorian-era gentlemen's club (it was built in the 1880s). Slip into a booth beneath the original chandeliers and sample the traditional English grub. *41 Mount St.* ☎ *0207/499-1843. Tube: Green Park. Map p 112.*

The mellow Admiral Duncan is a friendly place to down a pint.

★★★ Cittie of York BLOOMS-

BURY   There's been a pub on this site since 1430, and though the current building dates back "only" to the 1890s, there's still an old-world (faux) vibe, and (real) ale. Check out the churchlike interior and its immense wine vats. Closed Sunday. *22 High Holborn.* ☎ *0207/242-7670. Tube: Chancery Lane. Map p 113.*

★★ Coach & Horses SOHO   This

traditional Old English pub inspired Keith Waterhouse's popular play *Jeffrey Bernard Is Unwell.* The pub has character, has a friendly staff, and attracts an interesting crowd. *29 Greek St.* ☎ *0207/437-5920. Tube: Oxford Circus. Map p 112.*

★★ The Grenadier BELGRAVIA

This charming pub is tucked in a secluded mews. It's best known for its Sunday bloody marys, resident ghost, and historic military past (the Duke of Wellington's soldiers used it as their mess hall). *18 Wilton Row.* ☎ *0207/235-3074. Tube: Knightsbridge. Map p 115.*

★★ The Lamb BLOOMSBURY

You'll find one of the city's few remaining "snob screens"—used to protect drinkers from prying eyes—at this Victorian pub. Those who've enjoyed the anonymity here include the Bloomsbury Group and Charles Dickens. *98 Lamb's Conduit St.* ☎ *0207/405-0713. Tube: Russell Sq. Map p 113.*

★★ Museum Tavern BLOOMS-

BURY   This early-18th-century (and marketing-savvy) pub, the former Dog & Duck, changed its name when the British Museum was built across the street in the 1760s. The old-style decor remains intact. *49 Great Russell St.* ☎ *0207/242-8987. Tube: Russell Sq. Map p 112.*

★★★ **Nags Head** BELGRAVIA
This rarity, an independently owned pub, was built in the early 19th century for the posh area's working stiffs. A "no cellphones" rule attempts to keep the 21st century from intruding. *53 Kinnerton St.* ☎ *0207/235-1135. Tube: Knightsbridge. Map p 115.*

★★ **Old Bank of England** THE CITY This unusual pub is housed in a converted former bank that has retained all the majesty of a palace of finance, with a huge interior and wonderful murals. It's a City hangout, so it's closed on weekends. *194 Fleet St.* ☎ *0207/430-2255. Tube: Temple. Map p 116.*

★★ **Troubadour Café** EARL'S COURT Yes, it's a restaurant, but it's also a pub, a bar, and a bohemian hangout. There are poetry readings, live music, and singer-songwriter nights in its warren of warm little rooms. *265 Old Brompton Rd.* ☎ *0207/370-1434. www.troubadour.co.uk. Tube: Earl's Court. Map p 111.*

★★ **Williamson's Tavern** EAST END With a history that goes back to Londinium (there are excavated Roman tiles in the fireplace), this pub was once the home of the Lord Mayor of London and lies in an alley fronted by gates that were gifts of William III and Mary II. *1 Groveland Court.* ☎ *0207/248-6280. Tube: Mansion House. Map p 116.*

★★★ **Ye Olde Mitre Tavern** EAST END Good service, beamed ceilings, and the stump of a tree Queen Elizabeth I reportedly frolicked under make this historic treasure a must-see. It's hard to find, but do try. *Ely Court, off Ely Place.* ☎ *0207/405-4751. Tube: Chancery Lane. Map p 116.*

Bars
★★ **Abbaye** SOUTH KENSINGTON A mellow atmosphere and some truly outstanding beers make this European brasserie and bar a great hangout. Wash down some mussels with the great Belgian suds. *102 Old Brompton Rd.* ☎ *0207/373-2403. Tube: Gloucester Rd. Map p 114.*

★★ **Ain't Nothin' But? The Blues Bar** SOHO A blues joint plucked straight from the bayou; it may not be Bourbon Street, but there's good jambalaya, funky tables, and live blues every night of the week. Be prepared to wait in line on weekends. *20 Kingly St.* ☎ *0207/287-0514. www.aintnothin but.co.uk. Tube: Piccadilly Circus. Map p 112.*

The old-fashioned Nags Head in Belgravia.

★★ **BBar** VICTORIA This supertrendy bar with an African-inspired decor serves more than 60 cocktails. There's a vast wine cellar and a fusion menu of appetizing dishes. *43 Buckingham Palace Rd.* ☎ *0207/958-7000. www.bbarlondon.com. Tube: Victoria. Map p 112.*

★ **Beach Blanket Babylon** KENSINGTON Truly wacko decor (fireplace shaped like a tiger's mouth, a gangplank, and other kitschy excesses) will bring a smile to your lips that the often lousy service won't entirely wipe off. *5 Ledbury Rd.* ☎ *0207/229-2907. www.beachblanket.co.uk. Tube: Notting Hill Gate. Map p 111.*

★★ **Beduin Bar** FARRINGDON It's the height of sophistication, thanks to a stylish Moroccan Souk decor (red sofas, silver tables, and so on) spread out over three floors. *57–59 Charterhouse St.* ☎ *0207/336-4484. www.beduin-london.co.uk. Tube: Farringdon. Map p 116.*

★ **Blue Bar** KNIGHTSBRIDGE In the lovely Berkeley Hotel, this tiny (50-person) and, yes, blue (Luyten's blue, to be exact) bar serves 50 varieties of whisky and tapas-type snacks to a very upscale crowd. *Wilton Place.* ☎ *0207/235-6000. www.the-berkeley.co.uk. Tube: Hyde Park Corner. Map p 115.*

★★ **Canal 125** ISLINGTON Overlooking Regent's Canal, this three-floor Moroccan-themed bar has a great atmosphere and sexy decor, a selection of imaginative and traditional cocktails, and tasty English food. DJs spin tunes on weekends. *125 Caledonian Rd.* ☎ *0207/837-1924. www.canal125.co.uk. Tube: King's Cross. Map p 113.*

★★★ **Dorchester Bar** MAYFAIR The mega-expensive hotel's bar is awash in lacquered mahogany and velvet, red glass stalagmites, and

Down a whisky at the Berkeley Hotel's elegant Blue Bar.

mirrored tables. The vast selection of spirits and cocktails boasts more vermouth than any other bar in the U.K. *53 Park Lane.* ☎ *0207/629-8888. www.thedorchester.com. Tube: Hyde Park Corner. Map p 112.*

★★★ **The Edge** SOHO This four-floor gay and lesbian club caters to a diverse crowd with a cafe, piano bar, lounge, dance floor, and plenty of colorful characters. *11 Soho Sq.* ☎ *0207/439-1313. Tube: Tottenham Court Rd. Map p 112.*

★★★ **G-A-Y Bar** SOHO In the center of Old Compton Street's "Gaysville," three floors filled with video screens and pop music cater to people of every sexual persuasion looking for fun. *30 Old Compton St.* ☎ *0207/494-2756. www.g-a-y.co.uk. Tube: Leicester Sq. Map p 112.*

★★★ **Green Carnation** SOHO Inspired by Oscar Wilde, this high-brow salon is lavish and classy. Upstairs is relaxed, downstairs more boisterous. I recommend the raspberry *caipiroska*, with vodka, fresh lime, crushed ice, and raspberries. *5 Greek St.* ☎ *0207/434-3323. www.greencarnationsoho.co.uk. Tube: Oxford Circus. Map p 112.*

★★★ **Guanabara** HOLBORN Chic Latin bar where Brazilian artists

Sip a cocktail at The Library bar in the posh Lanesborough hotel.

play Latin cool, funk, samba, and Brazilian jazz in a spacious modern interior. Try one of the exotic, cutting edge cocktails. You won't be able to stand still. *Parker St., corner of Drury Lane.* ☎ *0207/242-8600. www.guanabara.co.uk. Tube: Holborn. Map p 113.*

★★ **Isola** KNIGHTSBRIDGE This upscale bar features floor-to-ceiling windows, well-dressed women, a decent wine list, and strong cocktails. *145 Knightsbridge.* ☎ *0207/838-1044. Tube: Knightsbridge. Map p 115.*

★★ **Janet's Bar** SOUTH KENSINGTON Owned by an expat, ex-lawyer Yankee (the eponymous Janet), this is a bar with attitude—it's very kitschy and a lot of fun. There's live music on Thursday, Friday, and Saturday nights. *30 Old Brompton Rd.* ☎ *0207/581-3160. Tube: S. Kensington. Map p 115.*

★★★ **The Library** KNIGHTSBRIDGE Lots of business execs on expense accounts sip cocktails and cognac at this sophisticated and atmospheric bar in the Lanesborough hotel. A roaring fire and tinkling piano keys complete the picture. *1 Lanesborough Place.* ☎ *0207/259-5599. Tube: Hyde Park Corner. Map p 115.*

★★★ **Mephisto** MAIDA VALE Taking its name from Goethe's *Faus* (and the Marvel comic book series), this basement bar is a devilishly louche hangout. Resident DJs play '80s pop rock and indie classics amidst a cozy atmosphere marked by candles and slouchy sofas. *254 Edgeware Rd.* ☎ *0207/724-9436. www.mephistobar.co.uk. Tube: Edgeware Rd. Map p 115.*

★★ **93 Feet East** SHOREDITCH Great DJs spin funk, hip-hop, disco, rock, and indie in a large space that includes a main bar with a stage for live music, an intimate gallery bar with bench seating, and a pink bar with comfy sofas. *150 Brick Lane.* ☎ *0207/247-3293. www.93feeteast co.uk. Tube: Aldgate E. Map p 116.*

★★ **Noble Rot** MAYFAIR Although it becomes a members-only club after 10pm, come here for dinner and you might get to stay for the stylish bar scene, featuring a who's who of posh young London. *3–5 Mill St.* ☎ *0207/629-8877. Tube: Oxford Circus. Map p 112.*

★★★ **Proud Bar** CAMDEN Situated in a 200-year-old horse hospital, this immense bar, photo gallery, and music venue is achingly hip and visually stunning. The gig room hosts megastars such as Amy Winehouse; the huge outdoor terrace makes it the perfect summer venue *Stables Market, Chalk Farm Rd.* ☎ *0207/424-3867. www.atproud. net. Tube: Chalk Farm. Map p 112.*

★★★ **The Rivoli Bar** WEST END The Ritz Hotel's restored Art Deco bar offers all the atmosphere you would expect from this bastion of over-the-top swank, as well as a varied menu of expensive drinks. A strict dress code keeps the young at bay. *150 Piccadilly.* ☎ *0207/493-8181. Tube: Green Park. Map p 112.*

★★ **The Soho** SOHO   Small cave-like booths create an intimate atmosphere at this cozy basement bar, which serves superb cock-tails—try the Raspberry Bellini. The dance floor is small, but who cares when the DJs are so great. *12–13 Greek St.* ☎ *0207/025-7844. www. thesohobar.co.uk. Tube: Oxford Circus. Map p 112.*

★★ **Sports Café** WEST END   When you've got to get your sports fix, this is the place to come: 120 TVs, seven pool tables, three bars, a dance floor, and four giant screens of games, games, and more games. *80 Haymarket.* ☎ *0207/839-8300. www.thesportscafe.net. Tube: Pic-cadilly Circus. Map p 112.*

★★★ **Vertigo 42** THE CITY   On the 42nd floor of a skyscraper, this bar is the highest in England and features splendid (and rare for Lon-don) views. It's the perfect place to sip a cocktail at sunset. *Tower 42, 25 Old Broad St.* ☎ *0207/877-7842. www.vertigo42.co.uk. Tube: Liver-pool St. Map p 116.*

★ **Waxy O'Connors** WEST END   This roaring Irish bar features mad Gaelic music, tipsy crowds, and a shameless sort of tourist appeal. The weird decor improves with each drink—you'll love the indoor tree. *14–16 Rupert St.* ☎ *0207/287-0255. www.waxyoconnors.co.uk. Tube: Leicester Sq. Map p 112.*

★★★ **Windows Bar** MAYFAIR   The best view of Hyde Park to be had is from this very chichi bar on the 28th floor of the London Hilton on Park Lane. Dress is strictly smart casual. *22 Park Lane.* ☎ *0207/493-8000. Tube: Hyde Park Corner. Map p 112.*

Dance Clubs & Live Music

★★★ **Aquarium** EAST END   This crazy but popular nightclub offers you the chance to doff your clothes and jump in a pool with strangers. Germaphobes may want to stick to the fully clothed drinking and danc-ing. *256 Old St.* ☎ *0207/251-6136. www.clubaquarium.co.uk. £8–£15 cover. Tube: Old St. Map p 116.*

★★★ **Bar Rumba** SOHO   An inti-mate basement venue with mood lighting and leather couches. The versatile club has drum & bass, R&B, hip-hop, salsa, and comedy nights. *36 Shaftsbury Ave.* ☎ *0207/287-6933. www.barrumba.co.uk. £3–£12 cover after 9pm. Tube: Leicester Sq. Map p 112.*

★ **Chinawhite** WEST END   With oriental styles, exotic drapes, and satin cushions, this still-popular club may be slightly past its glitzy A-lis-ters-only heyday, but it still pulls in the members. E-mail **lists@vickib. co.uk** to get on the guest list Thurs-days and Fridays. *6 Air St.* ☎ *0207/ 343-0040. www.chinawhite.com. £15–£20 cover. Tube: Piccadilly. Map p 112.*

The London Hilton's Windows Bar offers beautiful views of Hyde Park.

The Best Nightlife

★★★ **Fabric** EAST END   A favorite with London's committed weekend partygoers and hot-off-the-press vinyl lovers. Dance till 5am to the drum & bass, electro, and techno beats on the "bodysonic" dance floor, where you can feel the music's vibrations through your feet. *77a Charterhouse St.* ☎ *0207/336-8898. www.fabriclondon.com. Tube: Farringdon. Map p 116.*

★★★ **Heaven** COVENT GARDEN   Proving no one does clubs better than gay revelers, this London landmark has 25 years of partying under its belt, and it's growing old disgracefully. *Under the Arches, Villiers St.* ☎ *0207/930-2020. www.heaven-london.com. £6–£15 cover. Tube: Embankment. Map p 113.*

★★ **Herbal** EAST END   In trendy Shoreditch, you'll find this dark and intimate club buzzing with two dance floors, the occasional celeb, and exotic music. Leave the suits at home; this is warehouse chic at its best. *12–14 Kingsland Rd.* ☎ *0207/* 613-4462. www.herbaluk.com. £5–£15 cover. Tube: Old St. Map p 116.

★★★ **Madame JoJo's** SOHO   This unpretentiously cool spot has a well-earned reputation as one of Soho's most fun clubs, with decent drink prices and a good dance floor. The nightly offerings range from live music to comedy to Saturday-night drag queens. *8–10 Brewer St.* ☎ *0207/734-3040. www.madame jojos.com. £5–£15 cover. Tube: Piccadilly. Map p 112.*

★★★ **Ministry of Sound** ELEPHANT & CASTLE   Housed in a converted warehouse with four bars, MOS has three huge dance floors (including The Box, which is painted black from floor to ceiling), flatscreen TVs, and a hefty sound system playing techno, hip-hop, funk, house, and garage. E-mail ahead to get on the guest list and skip the lengthy queue outside. *103 Gaunt St.* ☎ *0207/378-6562. www. ministryofsound.com. £15–£20 cover. Tube: Elephant & Castle. Map p 116.*

Heaven, a veteran London club, still packs in the crowds.

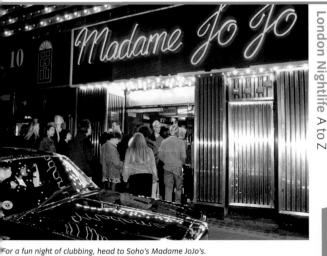

For a fun night of clubbing, head to Soho's Madame JoJo's.

★★★ **Opium** SOHO   This restaurant/club features a deluxe French-Vietnamese interior and bizarre cocktails of exotic provenance, such as plantain-infused rum. Eclectic menu, live music, and a stylish, rich crowd. *1a Dean St.* ☎ *0207/287-9608. £10–£15 cover. Tube: Tottenham Court Rd. Map p 112.*

★★ **Paragon Lounge** WEST END Popular with the young and moneyed, this Art Deco nightclub features live music, dancing, and Italian food. It's members-only after midnight, so get there early. *9 Hanover St.* ☎ *0207/355-3337. Tube: Oxford St. Map p 112.*

★★★ **Plastic People** EAST END For true music aficionados, the decidedly unpretentious P.P. offers live jazz, Latin, techno, soul, hip-hop, house, and funk. Ironically named, it attracts a casual, jovial crowd. *147–149 Curtain Rd.* ☎ *0207/739-6471. www. plasticpeople.co.uk. £8–£15 cover. Tube: Old St. Map p 116.*

★★★ **Ronnie Scott's** SOHO Open since 1959, this granddaddy of London's jazz clubs fully deserves its legendary reputation. The best jazz musicians in the world play this classy but relaxed venue every night. *47 Frith St.* ☎ *0207/439-0747. www.ronniescotts.co.uk. £20–£25 cover. Tube: Leicester Sq. Map p 112.*

★★★ **Sketch** MAYFAIR   Glitzy, glam, and riotously decorated, Sketch attracts celeb visitors and well-heeled regulars by successfully combining food, music, drinking, and art. *9 Conduit St.* ☎ *0870/ 777-4488. Tube: Oxford Circus. Map p 112.*

★★★ **The Social** FITZROVIA Civilized and unpretentious, this club hosts a casual, eclectic crowd, including the occasional celeb. Well-dressed dancers, an evening juke-box and late-night DJs, serious cocktails, and fun food. *5 Little Portland St.* ☎ *0207/636-4992. www.thesocial.com. Tube: Oxford Circus. Map p 112.*

London **Pub Crawl**

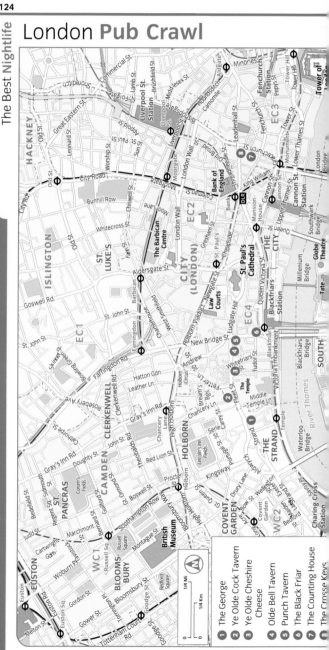

1. The George
2. Ye Olde Cock Tavern
3. Ye Olde Cheshire Cheese
4. Olde Bell Tavern
5. Punch Tavern
6. The Black Friar
7. The Counting House
8. The Crosse Keys

The public house, an institution that originated in London, was the place at the heart of a neighborhood where politics and gossip met with ale, beer, and coffee. Pubs doubled as post offices, inns, and gaming rooms, providing relaxation—and a chance to get rip-roaring drunk. Today's pubs still offer visitors a taste of the past along with a pint. This evening jaunt explores some of The City's best pubs and, like the intrepid explorers of the Empire, follows an eastward passage. START: **Temple Tube station**

1 ★★★ The George. When it opened in 1723, it was a coffee-house frequented by scribblers Horace Walpole, Oliver Goldsmith, and the ubiquitous Dr. Samuel Johnson. This traditional Victorian pub, set just across from the Royal Courts of Justice, still has beautiful if faux medieval timbering and stained glass. *213 The Strand.* ☎ *0207/353-9638. Map p 124.*

In good weather, you can eat outside at The George.

2 ★ Ye Olde Cock Tavern. The main reason to come to this so-so pub is its architecture: The cockerel was supposedly made by master carver Grinling Gibbons, and much of the building survived the Great London Fire and dates back to the 16th century. It was a favorite of Dickens, Samuel Pepys, and Alfred Lord Tennyson (who mentioned it in one of his poems, a copy of which hangs near the entrance). Check out the occasional quiz night. *22 Fleet St.* ☎ *0207/353-8570. Map p 124.*

The historic Ye Olde Cheshire Cheese is reportedly haunted.

3 ★★★ Ye Olde Cheshire Cheese. This wonderfully atmospheric, labyrinthine old pub was rebuilt right after the fire of 1666 and hasn't changed much since. Dr. Samuel Johnson lived around the corner, and other literary ghosts haunt the place. *Wine Office Court, 145 Fleet St.* ☎ *0207/353-6170. Map p 124.*

4 ★★ Olde Bell Tavern. This cozy and authentic pub was built in the 1670s for the workmen constructing St. Bride's (the "wedding cake" church designed by Wren in 1670), and maintains an old-world ambience with its leaded windows and wainscoted walls. Its decor may not wow you, but this pub's laid-back and genial atmosphere makes it a good spot for a pint. Closed weekends. *95 Fleet St.* ☎ *0207/583-0216. Map p 124.*

5 ★★ **Punch Tavern.** Bearing the scars of an ownership feud that divided the premises in two, this Victorian pub was the place where *Punch* was founded in 1841; look for artifacts from that magazine (as well as *Punch & Judy*–themed memorabilia) on the walls. The bright interior features some beautifully etched mirrors and Art Nouveau chandeliers. Closed Sunday. *99 Fleet St.* ☎ *0207/353-6658. Map p 124.*

The historic Punch Tavern on Fleet Street.

6 ★★★ **The Black Friar.** The amazingly detailed interior of this wedge-shaped Arts and Crafts pub is a feast for the eye. The magnificently carved friezes of monks remind you that the pub was built on the site of a 13th-century Dominican monastery, and under the vaulted ceiling you'll find such inscribed thoughts as WISDOM IS RARE. It's a popular after-work watering hole for The City's business set. *174 Queen Victoria St.* ☎ *0207/236-5474. Map p 124.*

The Black Friar pub was built on the site of a medieval monastery.

7 ★★★ **The Counting House.** Oddly opulent despite its plain name, this must-see pub has a glass dome, a balcony (great for people-watching), extravagant chandeliers, gilded mirrors, and marbled walls. It looks more like a palace than a pub, but was actually a bank in a previous incarnation. *50 Cornhill St.* ☎ *0207/283-7123. Map p 124.*

8 ★★★ **The Crosse Keys.** Very grand, this former bank is now an elegant pub with three separate eating rooms, a courtyard, high ceilings, wonderful wall carvings, and glass domes. It's almost too stately to be a pub, but then the best thing about London pubs is their crazy variety. Closed Sunday. *9 Gracechurch St.* ☎ *0207/623-4824. Map p 124.* ●

Arts & Entertainment Best Bet

Best for a Laugh
★★★ Comedy Cafe, *66–68 Rivington St. (p 133)*

Best for Opera
★★★ Royal Opera House, *Covent Garden (p 133)*

Best Baroque Concerts
★★★ St. Martin-in-the-Fields Evening Candlelight Concerts, *Trafalgar Sq. (p 132)*

Best Restored Theater
★★★ Royal Albert Hall, *Kensington Gore (p 132)*

Most Comfortable Movie Theater Seats
★★★ Electric Cinema, *191 Portobello Rd. (p 134)*

Best for a Cheap Movie Date
★★★ Prince Charles Cinema, *7 Leicester Place (p 134)*

Most Old-Fashioned Cinema
★★★ Coronet Cinema, *Notting Hill Gate (p 134)*

Best Free Live-Music Performances
★★ St. James's Piccadilly, *197 Piccadilly (p 132)*

Best for Independent Films
★★ Curzon Mayfair, *38 Curzon St. (p 134)*

Best Concert Venue
★★★ Indigo2 at the O2 Arena, *Peninsula Sq. (p 132)*

Best Outdoor Performances
★★ Open Air Theatre, *Inner Circle, Regent's Park (p 135)*

Best Ballet
★★★ Sadler's Wells, *Rosebery Ave. (p 133)*

Previous page: For truly authentic stagings of the Bard's plays, attend a performance at Shakespeare's Globe Theatre.

Best Symphony
★★★ London Symphony Orchestra at the Barbican Centre, *Silk St. (p 132)*

Best Modern Dance
★★ The Place, *17 Duke's Rd. (p 133)*

Best New Playwrights
★★★ Royal Court Theatre, *Sloane Sq. (p 135)*

Best Shakespeare
★★★ Shakespeare's Globe Theatre, *New Globe Walk (p 135)*

Best Theatrical Repertory Company
★★★ Royal National Theatre, *S. Bank (p 135)*

Longest Running Musical
★★★ Les Miserables, *Queen's Theatre (p 136)*

The Royal Court Theatre has been staging cutting edge drama since the days of George Bernard Shaw.

West End **Theaters**

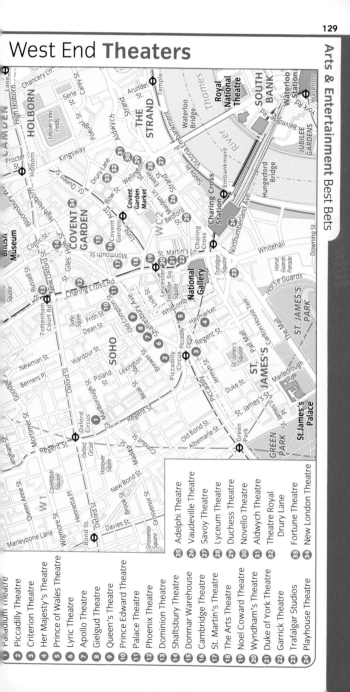

1. Palladium Theatre
2. Piccadilly Theatre
3. Criterion Theatre
4. Her Majesty's Theatre
5. Prince of Wales Theatre
6. Lyric Theatre
7. Apollo Theatre
8. Gielgud Theatre
9. Queen's Theatre
10. Prince Edward Theatre
11. Palace Theatre
12. Phoenix Theatre
13. Dominion Theatre
14. Shaftsbury Theatre
15. Donmar Warehouse
16. Cambridge Theatre
17. St. Martin's Theatre
18. The Arts Theatre
19. Noel Coward Theatre
20. Wyndham's Theatre
21. Duke of York Theatre
22. Garrick Theatre
23. Trafalgar Studios
24. Playhouse Theatre
25. Adelphi Theatre
26. Vaudeville Theatre
27. Savoy Theatre
28. Lyceum Theatre
29. Duchess Theatre
30. Novello Theatre
31. Aldwych Theatre
32. Theatre Royal Drury Lane
33. Fortune Theatre
34. New London Theatre

London **Arts & Entertainment**

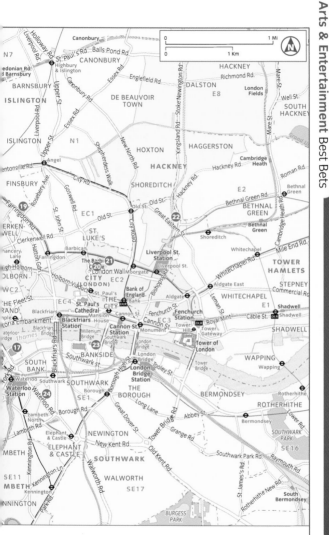

Prince Charles Cinema **12**
Royal Albert Hall **2**
Royal Court Theatre **4**
Royal Festival Hall **16**
Royal National Theatre **17**
Royal Opera House **18**
Sadler's Wells **19**
Shakespeare's Globe Theatre **23**
St. James's Piccadilly **9**
St. Martin-in-the-Fields **14**
The Place **8**
Wigmore Hall **6**

London A&E A to Z

Classical & Popular Music

★★★ Barbican Centre THE CITY
A gargantuan modern venue whose acoustics make it the best place for hearing music in the U.K. It's home to the first-class London Symphony Orchestra, which plays some 90 concerts here every year. *Silk St.* ☎ *0207/638-8891. www.barbican. org.uk. Tickets £10–£30. Tube: Barbican. Map p 131.*

★★ London Coliseum WEST END Converted into an opera house in 1968, London's largest theater is home to the English National Opera. Productions range from Gilbert and Sullivan to more challenging modern fare; most are staged in English. *St. Martin's Lane.* ☎ *0207/632-8300. www.eno.org. Tickets £10–£75. Tube: Charing Cross. Map p 130.*

★★★ O2 Arena & Indigo2 Room GREENWICH The massive interior of the previously underused Millennium Dome is now the most modern entertainment venue in England. Alongside the 20,000-seat arena is a smaller concert hall, the Indigo2, with perfect acoustics and comfortable seats. *Peninsula Sq.* ☎ *0208/463-2000. www.theo2.co.uk. Tickets £10–£150. Tube: N. Greenwich.*

★★★ Royal Albert Hall KENSINGTON This splendid Victorian pleasure palace is best known as the home of the city's annual Henry Wood Promenade Concerts (the Proms) in summer, when you'll hear orchestral classics and chamber music. *Kensington Gore.* ☎ *0207/ 589-8212. www.royalalberthall.com. Tickets £10–£80. Tube: Kensington High St. Map p 130.*

★★★ Royal Festival Hall SOUTH BANK More than 150,000 hours of

Royal Albert Hall hosts the Proms.

music have been performed at this acoustically exceptional complex since it opened in 1951. The hall's many free and low-priced concerts make it a great bet for those on a budget. *Belvedere Rd.* ☎ *0870/401- 8181. www.southbankcentre.co.uk. Tickets £7–£55. Tube: Waterloo. Map p 131.*

★★ St. James's Piccadilly ST. JAMES This gorgeous old Wren-designed church hosts 50-minute lunchtime classical recitals (Mon, Wed, and Fri at 1pm—a donation of £3 is suggested) and evening concerts as well. *197 Piccadilly.* ☎ *0207/381-0441. www.st-james- piccadilly.org. Tickets free–£19. Tube: Piccadilly. Map p 130.*

★★★ St. Martin-in-the-Fields WEST END Follow (allegedly) in Mozart's footsteps, and attend a concert at this atmospheric, newly refurbished church. Admission to its popular lunchtime concerts (Mon, Tues, and Fri at 1pm) is by suggested donation (£3.50). The candlelit evening musicales are one of London's best deals. *Trafalgar Sq.*

☎ 0207/839-8362. www.stmartin-in-the-fields.org. Tickets £6–£24. Tube: Charing Cross. Map p 130.

★★★ **Wigmore Hall** MARYLE-BONE Bechstein Pianos built this grand Renaissance-style recital hall—one of the world's finest—in 1901. The greatest names in classical music have taken advantage of this venue's fabulous acoustics. 36 Wigmore St. ☎ 0207/935-2141. www.wigmore-hall.org.uk. Tickets £8–£26. Tube: Bond St. Map p 130.

Comedy
★★ **Amused Moose Soho** SOHO Situated beneath a popular gay bar, this Thursday-through-Saturday comedy club has showcased such epic knee-slappers as Eddie Izzard. Moonlighting, 17 Greek St. ☎ 0207/341-1341. www.amused moose.co.uk. Tickets £8–£10. Tube: Leicester Sq. Map p 130.

★★★ **Comedy Cafe** EAST END Crowded tables and exposed brick walls provide an appropriate setting for raw comedy and plenty of heckling. There's a happy hour from 6 to 7pm. Closed Sunday to Tuesday. 66–68 Rivington St. ☎ 0207/739-5706. www.comedycafe.co.uk. Tickets £8–£15. Tube: Old St. Map p 131.

★★ **The Comedy Pub** SOHO This late-night venue (till 2am) serves good pub food and features

St. Martin-in-the-Fields.

comedy duos, troupes, and occasionally bizarre comedic routines. There's karaoke, too. 7 Oxendon St. ☎ 0207/839-7261. Tickets Free–£15. Tube: Piccadilly. Map p 130.

Dance
★★ **The Place** BLOOMSBURY Dedicated to both the teaching and the performing of dance, this small venue is the place in London to see contemporary new artists and startling modern dance. 17 Duke's Rd. ☎ 0207/121-1100. www.theplace. org.uk. Tickets £7–£17. Tube: Euston. Map p 130.

★★★ **Royal Opera House** COVENT GARDEN The brilliantly restored 19th-century ROH houses the even more brilliant Royal Ballet, a company on a par with the world's best. You can catch any number of classics, such as Giselle or Sleeping Beauty, but you'll pay for the privilege. Covent Garden. ☎ 0207/304-4000. www.royaloperahouse.org. Tickets £6–£165. Tube: Covent Garden. Map p 130.

★★★ **Sadler's Wells** ISLINGTON The best dance troupes in the world—from cutting edge to classical—are delighted to perform at this chic theater, where they are assured of modern facilities and an appreciative audience. Rosebery Ave. ☎ 0207/863-8198. www.sadlers wells.com. Tickets £10–£38. Tube: Angel. Map p 131.

The Royal Opera House.

The Electric Cinema is one of London's best art-house theaters.

Movies

★★★ Coronet Cinema NOTTING

HILL London's oldest-operating (and reputedly haunted) cinema first opened in 1923, and its lovely balcony has been seating popcorn throwers ever since. Half-price on Tuesday. *Notting Hill Gate.* ☎ *0207/727-6705. www.coronet cinema.co.uk. Tickets £7. Tube: Green Park. Map p 130.*

★★ Curzon Mayfair MAYFAIR

This historic art-house theater (it dates back to 1934) has been modernized and is famous for screening first-run films by Europe's finest filmmakers. *38 Curzon St.* ☎ *0207/495-0500. www.curzoncinemas.com. Tickets £9. Tube: Green Park. Map p 130.*

★★★ kids The Electric Cinema

NOTTING HILL Couches and leather seats, cocktails and yummy treats, Sunday double features, and a weekly mom-and-baby screening make this art house a destination

theater. Mainstream and independent films are shown. *191 Portobello Rd.* ☎ *0207/908-9696. www.electric cinema.co.uk. Tickets £9–£20. Tube: Ladbroke Grove. Map p 130.*

★★★ Prince Charles Cinema

SOHO One of London's best movie bargains, this independent theater offers singalong sessions of classic musicals, cult hits, mainstream classics, and first-run foreign flicks. *7 Leicester Place.* ☎ *0901/272-7007. www.princecharlescinema.com. Tickets £1.50–£5. Tube: Leicester Sq. Map p 130.*

Theater

★★★ Old Vic Theatre South-

bank SOUTHBANK Except for a few wartime interruptions, this venerable theater has been in continuous operation since 1818. The repertory troupe at "the actors' theatre" has included a veritable who's who of thespians over the years, including Sir Laurence Olivier, Dame Maggie Smith, and the Redgrave clan. *The Cut.* ☎ *0870/060-6628. www.oldvictheatre.com. Tickets £15–£48. Tube: Waterloo. Map p 131.*

A statue at the Barbican Center, home of the Royal Shakespeare Company.

Buying Theater Tickets

You can buy advance tickets for most of London's entertainment venues through the theaters' websites or through **Ticketmaster** (www.ticketmaster.co.uk). Expect to pay a booking fee as high as £3.50 per ticket. Some concierges can set aside theater tickets for hotel guests, so ask when booking your room.

For same-day, half-price tickets, your best bet is the **TKTS booth** (www.officiallondontheatre.co.uk) in the Clock Tower on the south side of Leicester Square, which opens at noon. Two boards list the day's available West End shows. The blockbusters will probably be MIA, but decent seats at all the longer-running productions should be available. Many theaters sell their own half-price standby tickets at the box office about an hour before curtain time.

Last Minute (www.lastminute.com) has scads of good deals on theater-dinner packages, but read the fine print carefully—some may have restrictions and booking fees that add up to more than £10.

★★★ Open Air Theatre

MARYLEBONE   The setting is idyllic, and the seating and acoustics are excellent at this Regent's Park venue. Presentations are mainly of Shakespeare's plays, usually in period costume. The season runs from June to mid-September. *Inner Circle, Regent's Park.* ☎ *0870/060-1811. www.openairtheatre.org. Tickets £8.50–£38. Tube: Baker St. Map p 130.*

★★★ Royal Court Theatre

CHELSEA   This leader in provocative, cutting edge theater is home to the English Stage Company, which was formed to promote serious drama. *Sloane Sq.* ☎ *0207/565-5000. www.royalcourttheatre.com. Tickets £10–£25. Tube: Sloane Sq. Map p 130.*

★★★ Royal National Theatre

SOUTH BANK   Home to one of the world's greatest stage companies, the Royal National presents the finest in world theater, from classic drama to award-winning new plays, comedies, and musicals. *South Bank.* ☎ *0207/452-3000. www.nationaltheatre.org.uk. Tickets £10–£40. Tube: Waterloo or Charing Cross. Map p 131.*

★★★ Shakespeare's Globe Theatre

SOUTH BANK   This outdoor theater is a replica of the Elizabethan original, with wooden benches (you can rent a cushion) and thatched galleries. It's the perfect spot to watch the Bard's works. *New Globe Walk, Bankside.* ☎ *0207/902-1400. www.shakespeares-globe.org. Tickets £5 groundlings, £12–£33 gallery seats. Tube: Blackfriars. Map p 131.*

West End Theaters

1 Adelphi Theatre, Strand. ☎ 0870/895-5598

2 Aldwych Theatre, 49 Aldwych. ☎ 0870/400-0805

3 Apollo Theatre, 39 Shaftesbury Ave. ☎ 0870/830-0200

4 The Arts Theatre, 6–7 Great Newport St. ☎ 0844/847-1608

5 Cambridge Theatre, Earlham St. ☎ 0870/890-1102

6 Criterion Theatre, Piccadilly Circus. ☎ 0870/060-2313

7 Dominion Theatre, 268–269 Tottenham Court Rd. ☎ 0870/169-0116

8 Donmar Warehouse, 41 Earlham St. ☎ 0870/060-6624

9 Drury Lane Theatre Royal Drury Lane, Drury Lane. ☎ 0870/890-6002

10 Duchess Theatre, Catherine St. ☎ 0844/412-4659

11 Duke of York Theatre, 104 St. Martin's Lane. ☎ 0870/060-6623

12 Fortune Theatre, Russell St. ☎ 0870/060-6626

13 Garrick Theatre, 2 Charing Cross Rd. ☎ 0870/040-0083

14 Gielgud Theatre, Shaftesbury Ave. ☎ 0844/482-5130

15 Her Majesty's Theatre, Haymarket. ☎ 0870/890-1106

16 Lyceum Theatre, 21 Wellington St. ☎ 0870/243-9000

17 Lyric Theatre, Shaftesbury Ave. ☎ 0870/890-1107

18 New London Theatre, Parker St. ☎ 0870/890-0141

19 Noel Coward Theatre (prev. Albery), 85 St. Martin's Lane. ☎ 0870/950-0920

20 Novello Theatre (prev. Strand), Aldwych. ☎ 0844/482-5170

21 Palace Theatre, 109–113 Shaftesbury Ave. ☎ 0870/890-0142

22 Palladium Theatre, 8 Argyll St. ☎ 0870/890-1108

23 Phoenix Theatre, 110 Charing Cross. ☎ 0870/060-6629

24 Piccadilly Theatre, Denman St. ☎ 0844/412-6666

25 Playhouse Theatre, Northumberland Ave. ☎ 0870/060-6631

26 Prince Edward Theatre, 28 Old Compton St. ☎ 0844/482-5151

27 Prince of Wales Theatre, Coventry St. ☎ 0870/850-0393

28 Queen's Theatre, Shaftesbury Ave. (at Cambridge Circus). ☎ 0870/950-0930

29 St. Martin's Theatre, West St. ☎ 0207/836-1443

30 Savoy Theatre, Savoy Court, Strand. ☎ 0870/164-8787

31 Shaftesbury Theatre, 210 Shaftesbury Ave. ☎ 0207/379-5399

32 Trafalgar Studios 2 Theatre (prev. Whitehall), 14 Whitehall. ☎ 0207/321-5400

33 Vaudeville Theatre, 404 Strand. ☎ 0870/890-0511

34 Wyndhams Theatre, Charing Cross Rd. ☎ 0870/950-0920 ●

Hotel Best Bets

A marble bathroom at the Dorchester.

Best **Historic Hotel**
★★★ Hazlitt's 1718 $$$$ *6 Frith St., W1 (p 149)*

Best **Hotel for Victoriana**
★★★ The Gore $$$$ *189 Queen's Gate, SW7 (p 148)*

Best **Size for Your Money**
★★ The Westland Hotel $$ *154 Bayswater Rd., W2 (p 152)*

Best **Luxury Hotel**
★★★ Claridge's $$$$$ *Brook St., W1 (p 146)*

Most **Refined Atmosphere**
★★★ The Connaught $$$$$ *16 Carlos Place, W1 (p 147)*

Best **Hotel for Royal Watching**
★★★ The Rubens at the Palace $$$ *39 Buckingham Palace Rd., SW1 (p 151)*

Best **Base for Museum-Hopping**
★★ The Gallery $$ *8–10 Queensberry Place, SW7 (p 148)*

Previous page: The Lanesborough is just one of the many luxe hotels that call London home.

Best **Views of the Thames**
★★ Park Plaza County Hall $$$ *1 Addington St., SE1 (p 150)*

Best **Chance to Get a Good Package Deal**
★★ The Rembrandt Hotel $$$ *11 Thurloe Place, SW7 (p 151)*

Most **Intimate Hotel**
★ Gate Hotel $ *6 Portobello Rd., W11 (p 148)*

Best **Hotel for Afternoon Tea**
★★★ The Goring Hotel, $$$$ *Beeston Place, SW1 (p 148)*

Best **Value**
★★ Mowbray Court Hotel $ *28–32 Penywern Rd., SW5 (p 150)*

Best **Boutique Hotel**
★★★ The Haymarket Hotel $$$$ *1 Suffolk Place, SW1 (p 148)*

Best **B&B**
★★ The Claverley $$ *13–14 Beaufort Gardens, SW3 (p 147)*

Best **Family Hotel**
★★ Lord Jim Hotel $ *23–25 Penywern St., SW5 (p 150)*

Most **Romantic Hotel**
★★★ San Domenico House $$$$ *29–31 Draycott Place, SW3 (p 151)*

Most **Quirky Decor**
★★★ Miller's Residence $$$ *111a Westbourne Grove, W2 (p 150)*

Best **Bathrooms**
★★★ The Dorchester $$$$$ *53 Park Lane, W1 (p 148)*

Best **Business Hotel**
★★ The Chamberlain Hotel $$$ *130–135 Minories, EC3 (p 146)*

Best **for Theater Buffs**
★★ Thistle Piccadilly $$$$ *Coventry St., W1 (p 152)*

East End Hotels

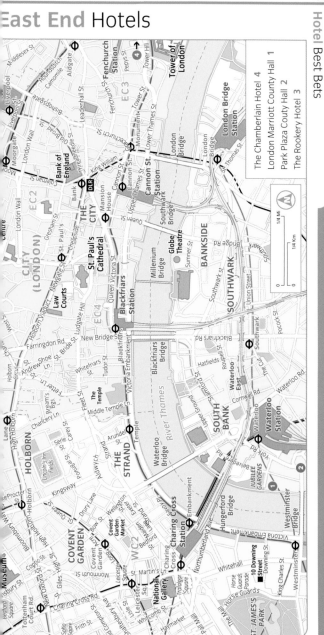

Kensington Hotels

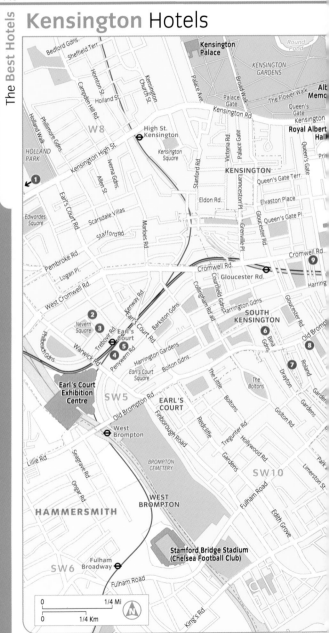

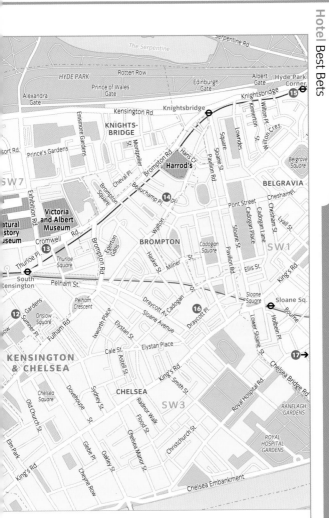

Notting Hill Hotels

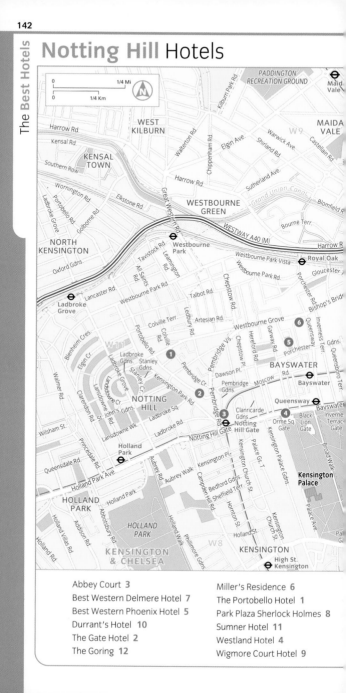

Abbey Court **3**
Best Western Delmere Hotel **7**
Best Western Phoenix Hotel **5**
Durrant's Hotel **10**
The Gate Hotel **2**
The Goring **12**

Miller's Residence **6**
The Portobello Hotel **1**
Park Plaza Sherlock Holmes **8**
Sumner Hotel **11**
Westland Hotel **4**
Wigmore Court Hotel **9**

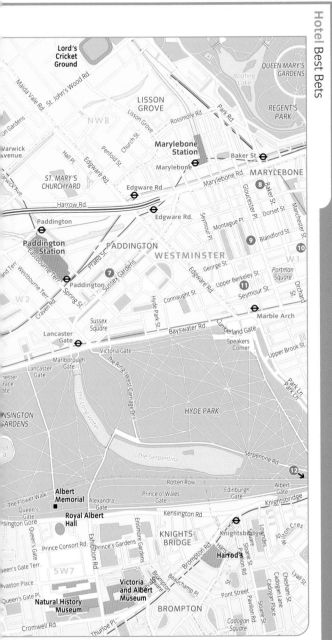

West End Hotels

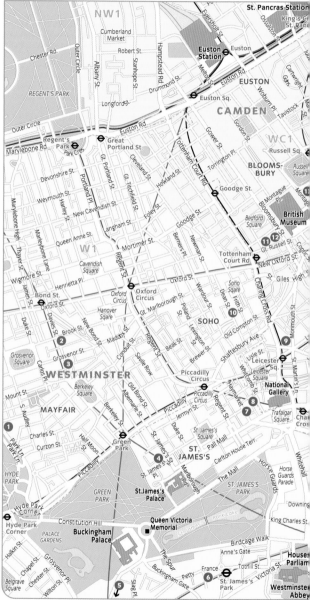

Claridge's **2**
The Connaught **3**
Covent Garden Hotel **9**
The Dorchester **1**
Hazlitt's **10**
Haymarket Hotel **7**
Jolly Hotel St Ermins **6**
Jury's Great Russell
Street Hotel **11**
The Montague on
the Gardens **14**

Morgan Hotel **12**
Royal Adelphi Hotel **17**
The Rubens
at the Palace **5**
The Ruskin Hotel **13**
The Stafford Hotel **4**
The Strand Palace **16**
Thistle Piccadilly **8**
Travelodge
Covent Garden **15**

London Hotels A to Z

★★ **kids** **Abbey Court** NOTTING HILL This four-floor Victorian town house has considerable charms, if you can get along without an elevator. *20 Pembridge Gardens, W4.* ☎ *0207/221-7518. www.abbey courthotel.co.uk. 22 units. Doubles £135–£185 w/breakfast. AE, DC, MC, V. Tube: Notting Hill Gate. Map p 142.*

★★ **kids** **Best Western Delmere Hotel** PADDINGTON Housed in an enlarged Victorian town house, this property is centrally located, has a reasonably attractive decor, and offers good package deals. *130 Sussex Gardens, W2.* ☎ *0207/706-3344. www.bw-delmerehotel.co.uk. 36 units. Doubles £129–£149 w/breakfast. AE, DC, MC, V. Tube: Paddington. Map p 143.*

★★ **kids** **Best Western Phoenix Hotel** BAYSWATER You know what you're getting with Best Western, plus this one is in an area with good transportation, and within walking distance of several places of interest, including Hyde Park. *1–8 Kensington Garden Sq., W2.* ☎ *0207/229-2494. www.best western.co.uk. 125 units. Doubles £75–£90. AE, DC, MC, V. Tube: Bayswater. Map p 142.*

★★★ **Blakes** SOUTH KENSINGTON Still trendy after all these years, and still celebrated for its exotic and lavish decor. Alas, the prices do seem to get harder to swallow. *33 Roland Gardens, SW7.* ☎ *0207/370-6701. www.blakeshotels.com. 47 units. Doubles £311–£440. AE, DC, MC, V. Tube: Gloucester Rd. Map p 140.*

★★ **kids** **The Chamberlain Hotel** EAST END Business travelers love the easy access to the City, and Tower of London lovers couldn't be happier with the location of this

The Corfu Suite at Blakes hotel.

modern hotel in an old Georgian building. *130–135 Minories, EC3.* ☎ *0207/373-3232. www.fullers hotels.com. 64 units. Doubles £185–£260. AE, DC, MC, V. Tube: Tower Hill. Map p 139.*

★★ **kids** **The Cherry Court Hotel** PIMLICO They don't come much cheaper than this pleasant hotel, at least not with the same degree of cleanliness and comfort. *23 Hugh St., SW1.* ☎ *0207/828-2840. www.cherrycourthotel.co.uk. 12 units. Doubles £55–£80 w/breakfast. Add 5% for credit cards. AE, MC, V. Tube: Victoria. Map p 141.*

★★★ **kids** **Claridge's** MAYFAIR This redoubtable London institution, close to Bond Street's shopping, has been the final word in elegance for decades. Rooms are spacious and service is impeccable. *Brook St., W1.* ☎ *0207/629-8860. www.may bourne.com. 203 units. Doubles £658–£775. AE, DC, MC, V. Tube: Bond St. Map p 144.*

★★ **kids The Claverley** KNIGHTS-BRIDGE   A very popular, award-winning B&B around the corner from Harrods and within walking distance of Hyde Park. *13–14 Beaufort Gardens, SW3. ☎ 800/747-0398 in the U.S.; 0207/589-8541. www. claverleyhotel.co.uk. 33 units. Doubles £172–£254 w/breakfast. AE, DC, MC, V. Tube: Knightsbridge. Map p 141.*

★★★ **The Connaught** MAYFAIR   With all the stately grandeur of an old-style gentlemen's club, the Connaught is as gloriously dignified as the neighborhood around it. A major refurbishment has put modern touches in the grand old hotel. Go for tea if you can't afford the steep rates. *16 Carlos Place, W1. ☎ 0207/499-7070. www.maybourne.com. 123 units. Doubles £681–£716. AE, DC, MC, V. Tube: Bond St. Map p 144.*

★★★ **kids Covent Garden Hotel** SOHO   Big beds, relatively large rooms, and a deft English decor make this popular hotel one of the best in Soho. The downside: The neighborhood gets a bit rowdy at night and is touristy during the day. *10 Monmouth St., WC2. ☎ 0207/806-1000. www. firmdale.com. 50 units. Doubles £276–£387. AE, DC, MC, V. Tube: Covent Garden. Map p 144.*

★★ **kids Cranley Gardens Hotel** SOUTH KENSINGTON   Good prices in a great neighborhood. The decor is a bit faux country-house, but it's a cheerful and pleasant family-owned hotel made up of four lovely Victorian houses. *8 Cranley Gardens, SW7. ☎ 0207/373-3232. www.cranleygardenshotel.com. 85 units. Doubles £89–£99. AE, MC, V. Tube: Gloucester Rd. Map p 140.*

★★★ **kids The Cranley on Bina Gardens Hotel** SOUTH KENSING-TON   Very romantic (the classic decor is laid over gorgeous period details), this hotel boasts a rooftop terrace, high ceilings, and Zen-brand toiletries—all in a quiet but convenient location. *10–12 Bina Gardens, SW5. ☎ 0207/373-0123. www.the cranley.com. 39 units. Doubles £188–£317. AE, MC, V. Tube: Gloucester Rd. Map p 140.*

A London institution, Claridge's is renowned for its elegant public rooms.

★★★ The Dorchester MAYFAIR

This opulent gem welcomes kings and commoners with equal panache. Elegant decor, first-rate amenities, and to-die-for bathrooms. *53 Park Lane, W1.* ☎ *800/727-9820 in the U.S.; 0207/629-8888. www. dorchesterhotel.com. 250 units. Doubles £323–£505. AE, DC, MC, V. Tube: Hyde Park Corner. Map p 144.*

★★ kids Durrant's Hotel

MARYLEBONE   This clubby hotel offers good value and a great location close to Oxford Street's shopping and the Wallace Collection. *George St., W1.* ☎ *0207/935-8131. www.durrantshotel.co.uk. 92 units. Doubles £229–£264. AE, MC, V. Tube: Bond St. Map p 143.*

★★ kids The Gainsborough

SOUTH KENSINGTON   A stone's throw from the Natural History Museum, this hotel offers well-appointed rooms at a decent price. *7–11 Queensberry Place, SW7.* ☎ *0207/838-1700. www.hotel gainsborough.co.uk. 49 units. Doubles £125–£155 w/breakfast. AE, DC, MC, V. Tube: S. Kensington. Map p 140.*

An elegant four-poster suite at The Gainsborough in South Kensington.

★★ kids The Gallery Hotel

SOUTH KENSINGTON   This Victorian hotel's pluses include small but comfortable rooms with attractive marble bathrooms, and a great breakfast. *8–10 Queensberry Place, SW7.* ☎ *0207/970-1805. www.eeh. co.uk/Gallery/gallery.html. 37 units. Doubles £135–£165 w/breakfast. AE, DC, MC, V. Tube: S. Kensington. Map p 140.*

★ Gate Hotel NOTTING HILL

With only six rooms, you had better book ahead, as the good value and great location ensure full occupancy most of the time. *6 Portobello Rd., W11.* ☎ *0207/221-0707. www.gate hotel.co.uk. 6 units. Doubles £75–£90. MC, V. Tube: Notting Hill Gate. Map p 142.*

★★ kids The Gore SOUTH KENS-

INGTON   Every room inside this gorgeous re-creation of an early Victorian hotel is individually decorated with fine antiques. *189 Queen's Gate, SW7.* ☎ *0207/584-6601. www.gorehotel.co.uk. 48 units. Doubles £340–£399. AE, DC, MC, V. Tube: Gloucester Rd. Map p 140.*

★★★ kids The Goring PIMLICO

A stone's throw from Victoria Station, this hotel has the feel of a country house, with a big walled garden, charming public spaces, and excellent afternoon teas. *Beeston Place, SW1.* ☎ *0207/396-9000. www.goringhotel.co.uk. 71 units. Doubles £395–£512. AE, DC, MC, V. Tube: Victoria. Map p 143.*

★★★ kids Haymarket Hotel

WEST END   The Haymarket's location is perfect for West End fun, and the decor is worth dropping by to gawk at. It's not cheap, but neither is putting a fabulous pool in central London. *1 Suffolk Place, SW1.* ☎ *0207/470-4004. www.firmdale. com. 50 units. Doubles £293–£381. AE, MC, V. Tube: Piccadilly Circle. Map p 144.*

The antiques-filled lounge at trendy Miller's Residence in Notting Hill.

★★★ Hazlitt's 1718 SOHO

Favored by the literary set, the 18th-century-flavored Hazlitt's feels more like a boarding house than a hotel. There's no elevator. *6 Frith St., W1.* ☎ *0207/434-1771. www.hazlittshotel. com. 23 units. Doubles £240–£299. AE, DC, MC, V. Tube: Tottenham Court. Map p 144.*

★★★ High Road House Hotel

CHISWICK I include this hotel outside of Central London because the value for money is so high. Good-sized rooms that are beautifully appointed in soothing simplicity, and great public areas. *162 Chiswick High Rd., W4.* ☎ *0208/742-1717. www.highroadhouse.co.uk. 14 units. Doubles £164–£188. AE, DC, MC, V. Tube: Turnham Green. Map p 140.*

★★ kids Jolly Hotel St Ermins

WESTMINSTER Recently bought by the NH Hotel Group, it may get a name change, but nothing will alter the old-fashioned grandeur of the lobby (though the uninspiring rooms could do with an update). *2 Caxton St., SW1.* ☎ *0207/222-7888. www.nh-hotels.com. 280 units. Doubles £104–£258. AE, MC, V. Tube: St. James. Map p 144.*

★★ kids Jury's Great Russell Street Hotel BLOOMSBURY Excellent access to the British Museum, Oxford Street shopping, and the West End. Nice staff and pleasant decor make it a solid if unexciting home away from home. *16–22 Great Russell St., WC1.* ☎ *0207/347-1000. www. jurysdoyle.com. 170 units. Doubles £116–£293. AE, DC, MC, V. Tube: Tottenham Court. Map p 144.*

★★★ kids K + K Hotel George

KENSINGTON Part of a popular European chain, this is a good bet for elegance and convenience at an affordable rate (depending on season). Enjoy the garden when weather permits. *1–15 Templeton Place, SW5.* ☎ *0207/598-8700. www.kkhotels. com. 154 units. Doubles £152–£275. AE, DC, MC, V. Tube: Earl's Court. Map p 140.*

★★★ kids The Lanesborough

KNIGHTSBRIDGE Housed in a former hospital building, this grand Regency-style hotel features state-of-the-art amenities—and your very own butler. *Hyde Park Corner, SW1.* ☎ *0207/259-5599. www.lanesborough.com. 95 units. Doubles £395–£650. AE, DC, MC, V. Tube: Hyde Park Corner. Map p 141.*

★★ kids London Marriott County Hall SOUTH BANK You can't beat the views of Big Ben and Parliament from this historic hotel's rooms, though the prices are steep. *County Hall, SE1.* ☎ *0207/928-5200. www.marriotthotels.com. 186 units.*

Doubles £316–£386. AE, DC, MC, V. Tube: Waterloo. Map p 139.

★★ kids Lord Jim Hotel EARL'S COURT   Known for its attractive package deals, this budget hotel offers plainly but pleasantly decorated rooms; families will fit easily inside the bigger rooms. *23–25 Penywern St., SW5. ☎ 0207/370-6071. www.thelordsgroup.co.uk. 50 units. Doubles £75–£89 w/breakfast. AE, DC, MC, V. Tube: Earl's Court. Map p 140.*

★★★ kids Miller's Residence NOTTING HILL   Brimming with antiques, this well-regarded hotel sports a wild, rococo decor and a trendy neighborhood location. *111a Westbourne Grove, W2. ☎ 0207/243-1024. www.millersuk.com. 8 units. Doubles £176–£217 w/breakfast. AE, MC, V. Tube: Bayswater. Map p 142.*

★★ kids The Montague on the Gardens BLOOMSBURY   In the shadow of the British Museum, this deluxe, country-style hotel has a garden and a ton of amenities. *15 Montague St. ☎ 0207/637-1001. www.redcarnationhotels.com. 100 units. Doubles £287–£311. AE, DC, MC, V. Tube: Russell Sq. Map p 144.*

★★ kids Morgan Hotel BLOOMS-BURY   The family-run Morgan features well-kept Georgian-style rooms. It's an old favorite of Anglophiles who can't get enough of the nearby British Museum. *24 Bloomsbury St., WC1. ☎ 0207/636-3735. 21 units. Doubles £98–£130 w/breakfast. MC, V. Tube: Tottenham Court. Map p 144.*

★★ kids The Mowbray Court Hotel EARL'S COURT   This spotless budget hotel, run by a friendly Irish family, features basic rooms, some without private bathrooms. *28–32 Penywern Rd., SW5. ☎ 0207/370-2316. www.mowbraycourthotel.co.uk. 90 units. Doubles £76–£86 w/breakfast. AE, DC, MC, V. Tube: Earl's Court. Map p 140.*

★★ kids Number Sixteen SOUTH KENSINGTON   This modernized Victorian town-house hotel is popular with Americans, quiet, and in a fun neighborhood. *16 Sumner Place, SW7. ☎ 0207/589-5232. www.numbersixteenhotel.co.uk. 42 units. Doubles £193–£264. AE, DC, MC, V. Tube: S. Kensington. Map p 141.*

★★ kids Park Plaza County Hall Hotel WATERLOO   Can't beat this new hotel on the Thames for price, views, and amenities. The rooms are good-sized too. *1 Addington St., SE1. ☎ 0207/034-4820. www.parkplazacountyhall.com. 398 units. Doubles £154–£195. AE, DC, MC, V. Tube: Baker St. Map p 139.*

★★ kids Park Plaza Sherlock Holmes Hotel MARYLEBONE   This modern boutique hotel with large rooms is close to Regent's Park and Oxford Street but hardly Sherlockian in decor. *108 Baker St., W1. ☎ 0207/486-6161. www.parkplazasherlockholmes.com. 119 units. Doubles £154–£184. AE, DC, MC, V. Tube: Baker St. Map p 143.*

The lobby lounge at the modern Park Plaza County Hall.

★★★ The Portobello Hotel NOT-TING HILL   Sumptuously decorated guest rooms mark this trendy hotel—a hit with the music and modeling set—located near Portobello Road. *22 Stanley Gardens, W1.* ☎ *0207/727-2777. www.portobello-hotel. co.uk. 24 units. Doubles £195–£280 w/breakfast. AE, DC, MC, V. Tube: Notting Hill Gate. Map p 142.*

★★ kids The Rembrandt Hotel SOUTH KENSINGTON   This solid tourist hotel across from the V&A is popular with groups because of its package deals and many rooms. *11 Thurloe Place, SW7.* ☎ *0207/589-8100. www.sarova.com. 195 units. Doubles £245–£265 w/breakfast. AE, DC, MC, V. Tube: S. Kensington. Map p 141.*

★★★ The Rookery Hotel EAST END   A sure-footed evocation of a bygone era, the Rookery is set on the edge of The City; each room is individually decorated with rare antiques. *Peter's Lane, Cowcross St., EC1.* ☎ *0207/336-0931. www.rookery hotel.com. 33 units. Doubles £282–£346. AE, DC, MC, V. Tube: Farringdon. Map p 139.*

★ kids Royal Adelphi Hotel WEST END   It's a bit like a college dorm, with small, spartan rooms and no elevator, but what it lacks in charm it makes up for in value. *21 Villiers St., WC2.* ☎ *0207/930-8764. www.royaladelphihotel.co.uk. 47 units. Doubles £78–£98 w/breakfast. AE, DC, MC, V. Tube: Embankment. Map p 145.*

★★★ kids The Rubens at the Palace VICTORIA   Traditional English hospitality combined with the latest in creature comforts. The Royal Rooms have the most atmosphere. *39 Buckingham Palace Rd., SW1.* ☎ *877/955-1515 in the U.S.; 0207/834-6600. www.redcarnation.com. 161 units. Doubles £304–£374. AE, DC, MC, V. Tube: Victoria. Map p 144.*

The George I room, one of the Royal Rooms at the Rubens at the Palace.

★ kids The Ruskin Hotel BLOOMSBURY   This clean, friendly, no-frills B&B in an old town house is located opposite the British Museum. There's an elevator. *23–24 Montague St., WC1.* ☎ *0207/636-7388. 33 units. Doubles £73–£94 w/breakfast. AE, DC, MC, V. Tube: Russell Sq. Map p 144.*

★★★ San Domenico House CHELSEA   An exquisite hotel delivering divine Italian luxury at its most romantic and English-accented. *29–31 Draycott Place, SW3.* ☎ *0207/581-5757. www.sandomenicohouse. com. 16 units. Doubles £235–£310. AE, DC, MC, V. Tube: Sloane Sq. Map p 141.*

★★★ kids The Stafford Hotel MAYFAIR   This gorgeous 18th-century hotel, set in a grand old neighborhood, combines English country style with modern amenities. *St. James's Place, SW1.* ☎ *0207/493-0111. www.thestaffordhotel.co.uk. 81 units. Doubles £352–£470. AE, DC, MC, V. Tube: Green Park. Map p 144.*

★★ kids The Strand Palace COVENT GARDEN   This big old

A bedroom at the well-priced Sumner Hotel.

hotel is more utilitarian than deluxe in decor, but nevertheless offers solid quality and service. Ask for upgrades and special deals. *372 Strand, WC2.* ☎ *0207/379-4737. www.strandpalacehotel.co.uk. 783 units. Doubles £165–£185 w/breakfast. AE, DC, MC, V. Tube: Embankment. Map p 145.*

★★★ **Sumner Hotel** MARBLE ARCH   One of London's best small, reasonably priced hotels, the Sumner is well-loved by clued-in visitors. *54 Upper Berkeley St., W1.* ☎ *0207/723-2244. www.thesumner.com. 20 units. Doubles £152–£188 w/breakfast. AE, DC, MC, V. Tube: S. Kensington. Map p 143.*

★★ kids **Thistle Piccadilly** PICCADILLY   There's no better location for those who want to hit the theaters, clubs, and restaurants of the West End. Check the website for packages and promotions. *Coventry St., W1.* ☎ *0870/333-9118. www.thistlehotels.com. 92 units. Doubles £293–£387 w/breakfast. AE, DC, MC, V. Tube: Piccadilly. Map p 144.*

★ kids **Travelodge Covent Garden** COVENT GARDEN   It's in a dreadful building, but the rooms are clean and serviceable, and the neighborhood rocks. And what you'll save on lodging, you can spend at the theaters and cafes on Drury Lane. *10 Drury Lane, WC2.* ☎ *0207/208-9988. www.travelodge.co.uk. 163 units. Doubles £59–£105. AE, MC, V. Tube: Covent Garden. Map p 145.*

★★★ **Twenty Nevern Square** EARLS COURT   An elegant European-Asian decor, a full range of amenities, and a garden make this one of the more sumptuous B&Bs in London. *20 Nevern Sq., SW5.* ☎ *0207/565-9555. www.twenty nevernsquare.co.uk. 20 units. Doubles £129–£195 w/breakfast. AE, DC, MC, V. Tube: Earls Court. Map p 140.*

★★ kids **Westland Hotel** NOTTING HILL   The family-run Westland has a dedicated following and is clean, welcoming, and surprisingly spacious for the cost. *154 Bayswater Rd., W2.* ☎ *0207/229-9191. www.westlandhotel.co.uk. 32 units. Doubles £105–£138 w/breakfast. AE, MC, V. Tube: Notting Hill. Map p 142.*

★ kids **Wigmore Court Hotel** MARYLEBONE   Clean, friendly, and well located, the Wigmore Court is a favorite of the budget-conscious and is well-suited to family groups. *23 Gloucester Place, W1.* ☎ *0207/935-0928. www.wigmore-hotel.co.uk. 16 units. Doubles £89–£130 w/breakfast. MC, V. Tube: Marble Arch. Map p 143.* ●

The
Savvy Traveler

Before You Go

Government Tourist Offices
In the U.S.: Visit Britain, 551 Fifth Ave., 7th Floor, New York, NY 10176 (☎ 800/462-2748). **In Canada:** Visit Britain, 5915 Airport Rd., Suite 120, Mississauga, Ontario L4V 1T1 (☎ 905/405-1840). **In Ireland:** Visit Britain, 18–19 College Green, Dublin 2 (☎ 01/670-8000). **In Australia:** Visit Britain, Level 16, Gateway, 1 Macquarie Place, Sydney, NSW 2000 (☎ 029/377-4400). **In New Zealand:** Visit Britain, Fay Rich White Building, 151 Queen St., Auckland 1 (☎ 09/303-1446). The best place for information, regardless of your home country, is on the Web at **www.visitbritain.com**.

The Best Time to Go
Though prices are highest in spring and summer, the weather is best then, with only occasional showers. Sunny and warm August is a sensible time to visit because many Londoners go on vacation, hotel rates may drop, and London's notorious traffic lightens up. The only problem is all those tourists, looking for a genuine British experience, and a reduction in services (closed restaurants and the like). Fares are cheapest between November and March. The city's museum and theater scenes are in full swing in winter, but the city can get dark and chilly and bleak. September and early October can be gray and rainy, too, but most gardens are still in bloom.

Festivals & Special Events
For more information on London events, check out the following websites: *www.visitlondon.com, www. londontown.com, www.thisislondon. co.uk, www.timeout.com, www. virtual-london.com,* and *www. allinlondon.co.uk.*

JAN. The full-dress **Charles I Commemoration** (☎ 0870/751-5178) that marks the king's beheading is held on the last Sunday of the month. A must-see for history buffs.

FEB. **Chinese New Year** is celebrated in Soho's Chinatown with the requisite dancing lions and red confetti. The **Great Spitalfields Pancake Race** (www.myshoreditch. co.uk) on Shrove Tuesday (called Pancake Day in London) is a bizarre old tradition that combines tossed pancakes and teams of runners.

MAR. The month's best-loved events are boat races (**www.theboat race.org**): the **Head of the River Race** from Mortlake to Putney Bridge, and the **Oxford & Cambridge Boat Race** in the opposite direction. There are a number of good pubs and vantage points along the 6.5km (4-mile) stretch, but Hammersmith and Putney bridges are the best places to watch.

APR. Tens of thousands of people run the **London Marathon** (www. london-marathon.co.uk), and it's been growing steadily every year. The 42km (26-mile) course runs from Greenwich Park to St. James's Park. The best views are from Victoria Embankment.

MAY. A difficult ticket, the **Chelsea Flower Show** (☎ 0845/260-5000; www.rhs.org.uk) is a wonderful spectacle, with very creative garden displays.

JUNE. The **Royal Academy Summer Exhibition** (www.royalacademy. org.uk), the world's largest, displays the works of artists of every genre and caliber. **The Queen's Official Birthday** (Elizabeth II was actually born in Apr) is honored with a carriage ride, a gun salute, and the **Trooping of the Colours** at Horse

Guards Parade. On **London Gardens Squares Day,** a number of gardens available only to private key-holders are open to an envious public. **Royal Ascot** (www.ascot.co.uk) is the big social horse event of the year, a time when the upper classes dust off their chapeaus and take part in the old tradition of betting on horses while dressed to the nines. The **Lawn Tennis Championships at Wimbledon** (☎ 0208/944-1066; www.wimbledon.org) need no introduction, but you will need a very-hard-to-get ticket (see "Spectator Sports," later in this chapter).

JULY. **The Proms** (☎ 0207/589-8212; www.bbc.co.uk/proms), formally known as the BBC Sir Henry Wood Promenade Concerts, held in and outside Royal Albert Hall, are the annual joy of London's classical music lovers.

AUG. The **Notting Hill Carnival** (www.portowebbo.co.uk), one of the largest street festivals in Europe, is held in and around Portobello Road. Expect crowds, beer, and spicy Caribbean cuisine.

SEPT. During the 2-day **Open House** (www.londonopenhouse.org), hundreds of usually inaccessible architectural gems are opened to the public. Several hundred boats of every description ply the Thames from Richmond to Greenwich in the **Great River Race** (www.great riverrace.co.uk), which is less a race than a proud parade of maritime multiculturalism.

OCT. At the 125-year-old **Pearly Kings & Queens Harvest Festival** (☎ 0207/766 1100; www.pearly society.co.uk), the descendants of London's cockney costermongers (market traders) dress in costumes covered with pearly buttons and gather at a church service at St. Martin-in-the-Fields for charity—and to show off their button-sewing

prowess. Floats and carriages make their way from Mansion House to the Royal Courts of Justice and back again during **The Lord Mayor's Show** (www.lordmayorsshow.org).

NOV. **Guy Fawkes Night** commemorates the thwarted destruction of Parliament with bonfires and fireworks all over London. Book a couple of spins on the London Eye (p 12, **7**) after dark so you can see London's sky lit up from near and far.

DEC. For the horse-mad, there is no better fun than the **International Show-jumping Championships** (☎ 0207/370-8202; www.olympia showjumping.com) in Kensington.

The Weather

London's notorious (man-made) pea-soup fogs have long been eradicated, but a tendency toward showers and gray skies is ever-present—particularly November through March, when the sun shows its face only briefly. The weather can be fickle, and experiencing all four seasons in the span of a single day is common in all seasons. The general climate is relatively mild, never going much above 75°F (24°C) or below 40°F (4°C). There are no great extremes, except for a few unpleasant dog days in summer (when a temp of 80°F/27°C is considered a heat wave) and the rare freezing snowfall during the short, dark days of a bleak midwinter.

Useful Websites

- **www.visitbritain.com:** Great Britain's official tourist website features lots of useful information and trip-planning advice.

- **www.londontown.com:** The official London Tourist Board site offers specials on hotels, sells theater tickets, and has lots of useful information.

- **www.visitlondon.com:** London's official website features loads of information and lets you

LONDON'S AVERAGE TEMPERATURE & RAINFALL

	JAN	FEB	MAR	APR	MAY	JUNE
Daily Temp (°F)	43	44	50	55	63	68
Daily Temp (°C)	6	7	10	13	17	20
Avg. Rainfall (in/mm)	3/54	1.5/40	1.5/37	1.5/37	1.8/46	1.8/45

	JULY	AUG	SEPT	OCT	NOV	DEC
Daily Temp (°F)	72	70	66	57	50	44
Daily Temp (°C)	22	21	19	14	10	7
Avg. Rainfall (in/mm)	2.2/57	2.3/59	1.9/49	2.2/57	2.5/64	1.9/48

book hotels, buy discount passes, and more.

- **www.thisislondon.co.uk:** The *Evening Standard*'s website is a good source of current entertainment and restaurant information.

- **www.timeout.com:** The weekly magazine has cultural event listings, as well as information on entertainment, restaurants, and nightlife.

- **www.tfl.gov.uk:** London Transport's website is the source of information on London's public transportation system, including the Tube, buses, and ferries.

- **www.royal.gov.uk:** If you're a royal watcher, or are just looking for information, trivia, or anything else about the British royal family, direct your browser to this site.

- **www.streetmap.co.uk:** This site has detailed London street maps and directions to addresses. Specify "London Street" when searching.

How to Get the Best Airfare

Besides traveling during the off season, when you can usually get cheap fares and promotional specials directly from the airlines, try the following:

- **Book on the Web.** The "Big Three" online travel agencies—Expedia.com, Orbitz, and Travelocity—often feature discounted fares. Another good website for low airfares to London is **www.cheaptickets.com**. Note also that booking your ticket on the major airlines' websites will usually save you a small amount of cash.

- **Use a Consolidator.** Also known as a bucket shop, these agencies usually offer good international fare deals. Reputable consolidators include **Flights.com** (☎ 201/541-3867; www.flights.com); **STA Travel** (www.Statravel.com), which caters to students and those 25 and under; and **FlyCheap** (☎ 800/359-2432; www.flycheap.com).

- **Bid on a Flight.** If you're willing to give up some control over your flight details, use an opaque fare service such as **Priceline** (www.priceline.com; www.priceline.co.uk for Europeans) or **Hotwire** (www.hotwire.com). Both offer rock-bottom prices in exchange for travel on a "mystery airline" at a mysterious time of day. The mystery airlines are all major, well-known carriers, but your chances of getting an odd flight time or having to change planes are good.

Cellphones

The three letters that define much of the world's wireless capabilities are GSM (Global System for Mobiles), a big, seamless network that makes for easy cross-border cellphone use throughout Europe and dozens of other countries worldwide. You can make and receive calls in London, though you will accrue whopping roaming charges.

International visitors can buy a pay-as-you-go mobile phone at any phone store in London. This gives you a local number and minutes that can be topped up with phone cards that can be purchased at news agents. O2 and Vodaphone are the best service networks.

Your hotel may be able to rent you a cellphone while in London, though it won't be cheap; inquire before you arrive. North Americans can rent one before leaving home from **InTouch USA** (☎ **800/872-7626;** www.intouchglobal.com) or **RoadPost** (☎ **888/290-1606** or 905/272-5665; www.roadpost.com).

Car Rentals

In a word—don't. Driving in London is a royal pain and I strongly recommend against it. You're far better off sticking to public transportation when you take into account the congestion fee (a charge of £8 for entering an arbitrarily drawn—and very large—area of the city 7am–6:30pm), the dreadful traffic, the dearth of street parking, and the astronomically high price of petrol. If you still want to rent a vehicle, all major car-rental companies operate in the U.K., and cars can be picked up at any of the major airports.

Getting **There**

By Plane

Air Canada, American, British Airways, Continental, Delta, Northwest, United, and Virgin Atlantic Airways offer nonstop service from various locations in the U.S. and Canada to London's major airports. **Qantas** offers daily service to London from Sydney and Melbourne.

London is served by four airports. **London Heathrow Airport** (☎ 0870/000-0123 for flight information), located 24km (15 miles) west of London, offers the quickest access to the city. The fastest way into town is the **Heathrow Express** (☎ 0845/600-1515; www.heathrowexpress.com) train to Paddington Station (15 min.; £15). You can also take a cheaper ride on the Underground's Piccadilly Line into Central London (40 min.; £4). Black cabs cost roughly £50 to the center of the city.

Increasingly popular **Gatwick Airport** (☎ 0870/000-2468 for flight information) is 40km (25 miles) south of London. The fastest (and best) way to get to the city is via the **Gatwick Express** (☎ 0845/850-1530; www.gatwickexpress.com) trains to Victoria Station (30 min.; £17). A taxi ride into London usually takes an hour, and can cost more than £125.

Stansted (☎ 0870/000-0303) and **Luton** (☎ 0158/240-5100) airports handle mostly short-hop flights on bargain airlines (usually easyJet and Ryanair) from European and U.K. destinations. Both are more than 80km (50 miles) from London. To get from Stansted to the city, take a **Stansted Express** (☎ 0845/850-0150; www.stanstedexpress.com) train to Liverpool Street Station (45 min.; £15). From

Luton, take **Greenline bus no. 757** (☎ 0870/608-2608) to Victoria Station (1 hr. 39 min.; £13).

By Train

The **Eurostar** provides direct train service between Paris (2¼ hr.) or Brussels (2 hr.) and London's St. Pancras Station in King's Cross. In London, make reservations for Eurostar at ☎ 0870/518-6186. (Outside the U.K., call 44123/361-7575.) You can make advance train reservations from any country at **www.eurostar.com**. King's Cross/St. Pancras has six Underground line connections (Piccadilly, Circle, Hammersmith & City, Metropolitan, Northern, and Victoria), as well as overland trains connecting to the north and Scotland. Buses and taxis are readily available just outside the station.

National Rail (☎ 0845/748-4950; www.nationalrail.co.uk) trains connect just about every major city in the U.K. to one of London's major train stations (Charing Cross, Liverpool, Paddington, Victoria, King's Cross, Waterloo, and Euston), some of which also handle traffic arriving from various points in continental Europe. All major train stations in Central London have Underground stations and offer easy access to buses and taxis.

By Bus

Bus connections to Britain from the Continent, using the Channel Tunnel (Chunnel) or ferry services, are generally not very comfortable and take as long as 8 hours, but you can get a round-trip to Paris for as little as £50. Do check ahead to make sure your bus has a bathroom onboard; some do not. **National Express** (☎ 0870/580-8080; www.nationalexpress.com) long-haul buses traveling within the U.K. and to the continent generally use centrally located Victoria Coach Station as their terminus. The bus station is on the corner of Buckingham Palace Road and Elizabeth Street, a few minutes' walk from the main Victoria Station, serviced by British Rail and London Underground trains, and a stop on the Underground's District and Circle lines. Victoria Station has a taxi stand and is the terminus for many local city buses.

Getting **Around**

Discount Travel Passes

Explaining the prices and passes for London's public transport is a Byzantine exercise worthy of a Monty Python skit. Sorting though the various prices for 1-day, 3-day, and 7-day passes; the rules for different ages of children; prices with and without museum discount passes; peak and off-peak travel time; and the different costs of tickets among the outer travel zones in London is exceedingly complicated. Worse, the system is always trying new "improvements" in the vain hope of softening the blow of the basic £4 one-way Underground ticket in zones 1 through 6, even while plotting the latest fare increase. If you want the very latest prices, and the possibility of grasping the latest twist in pricing and discounted travel, settle in for a long read at the **Transport for London** website at **www.tfl.gov.uk**. You can also pick up the booklet given away at all Tube stations that attempts to explain it all.

One way to cut through all the variables is the efficient and penny-wise **Oyster Card,** a prepaid, reusable "smart" card that deducts he cost of a trip each time you touch your card to the yellow card reader found on all public transportation (including the Docklands Light Railway and National Rail). You pay a one-time, refundable charge of £3 for the plastic card, but you'll save that on your first few trips with the Oyster Card's discounted fares just £1.50 for a one-way, off-peak Tube trip in zones 1 and 2 is deducted from an Oyster card). They can be purchased at any Tube station or online. It is not necessary to register the card. To retrieve the £3 card cost plus any money left on it; simply present it at any Tube station and they will refund your money on the spot.

Another nice feature is that the Oyster Card tops out each day at a certain price: The cap on Oyster Card charges per day on buses is £3; on off-peak tube trips it's £4.80 (during peak times it's £6.50). According to an Oyster Card spokesperson, the Oyster Card costs 50p less per trip than the system's alternative unlimited-trip Travelcard. For more information, call **0870/849-9999** or check out **www.oystercard.com**.

London Transport's **Travelcards** offer unlimited use of buses, Underground, and British Rail services in Greater London, with no cap, and no need to factor in zone variables, or daily caps on fares. The **1-day Travelcard** costs £6.70 (£2 for kids), which means you save £1.30 on one round-trip on the Tube. A **3-day Travelcard** costs £20 adults, £6 kids 5 to 15; a **7-day Travelcard** is £43 for adults, £22 kids 5 to 15.

Up to 4 children age 16 and under, accompanied by a ticket-holding adult, may travel free. Kids 14 to 16 need a photo ID card, which can be purchased at a Tube station or online at either **www.tfl.gov.uk** or **www.londontravelpass.com**.

You can buy Travelcards and Oyster Cards at machines (using cash or credit card) in Underground stations, but if you want to get the best travel card for your particular needs, go to the ticket seller's window and discuss the various options. With luck you'll find one of the many public transport workers who are able and willing to walk you through the maze of public transport ticket choices.

Surf the very comprehensive London Transport website at **www.tfl.gov.uk** for more information on discount options.

By Underground
The world's first underground train (known today as the Underground or Tube) was born in London in 1863. Stifling, overpopulated cars, sudden mysterious stops, and arbitrary line closures make the Underground the sacred monster of London's commuters (though visitors often adore it—I know New Yorkers who prefer it to the Big Apple's subways). Love it or loathe it, it's the lifeblood of the city, and its 12 lines (plus the Docklands Light Railway to Greenwich) are usually the quickest way to get around the city.

All Tube stations are clearly marked with a red circle and blue crossbar. Routes are color-coded. The Tube runs daily, except Christmas, from 5:30am to 12:30am (until 11:30pm Sun), after which you must take a night bus or taxi. Fares start at £4 for a single journey within Zones 1 through 6 (the ones most frequented by travelers). Buy your ticket, Oyster, or Travelcard from a machine inside the Tube station (some of them take credit cards) or from a clerk at a ticket window; insert it into the turnstile; and then retrieve it and hold onto it—it must be reinserted into the turnstile or presented to a clerk when you exit the station at your destination or you'll pay a fine of £20; repeat offenders can get hit with as much as a £1,000 fine!

Study a Tube map (available at most major Underground stations) or consult the indispensable *London A to Z* street atlas (pick it up at any London bookstore or newsstand, and refer to it as the "A to Zed") to find the stop nearest your destination. Note that you may have to switch lines in order to get from one destination to another. For more information on the Tube, check out **www.tfl.gov.uk**.

By Bus

The city's bus system has many advantages over the Tube: With the bus lanes and the (slight) reduction in traffic from the city's congestion charge, aboveground travel is almost as efficient as the Underground, it costs half as much, and you get better views of the city. The city's red double-decker buses are a tourist attraction in their own right. Route maps are available at major Underground stations (Euston, Victoria, and Piccadilly Circus, to name a few) or online at **www.tfl.gov.uk**. You can also call a 24-hour hot line (☎ **0207/222-1234**) for schedule and fare information.

Fares start at £2 for Zones 1 and 2, with prices rising the farther out you travel from Central London. Oyster Cards and Travelcards are valid on buses. A single bus fare using the Oyster Card is only 90p peak time, and caps out at £3. Travelcards cap out at £3.50. A 1-day bus Travel pass costs £3.50, a 7-day is £13, and a booklet of Bus Saver tickets costs £6 for six single trips. Kids 15 and under ride free, but a photo bus pass is required for 14- and 15-year-olds. Most Central London buses require that you buy your bus ticket from a ticket machine at a bus stop before boarding; these machines take exact change only. If

there is no machine at your bus stop (a rarity in Central London), you can pay the driver or conductor in cash (use small bills or coins only).

Double-decker buses are entered from the front. Pay the driver with cash, show your bus ticket, or your Travelcard, or touch your Oyster Card to the card reader as you board.

Night buses are the only way to get around by public transport after the Tube stops operating. Be sure that there is an "N" bus listed on your bus stop's route or you'll wait in vain until morning.

The newer "bendy buses" are single-deckers with dual carriages. You may enter these from any open door, but you must touch your Oyster Card to one of the yellow card readers throughout the bus, or you will be fined £20 on the spot. Inspectors often board these buses to catch fare evaders.

By Taxi

All airport and train stations have well-marked areas for London's legendary black cabs, many of which are now colored with advertising, but are still the same distinctive model that holds five people. You can hail a taxi anywhere, on any street, except in certain no-stopping zones marked by white zigzag lines along the curb. Available taxis will have a lit sign on top of the cab. Taxis can also be requested by phone, but you will pay more.

Only black cabs, whose drivers have undergone rigorous training known as "the Knowledge," are allowed to cruise the streets for fares. Don't get into cruising minicabs, which can legally pick up only those passengers who have booked them by telephone. Black cabs have metered fares (minimum fare has remained at £2.20, even as the 3.2% increase in April 2008 pushes the average fare up to £10.57), and urcharges are assessed after 8pm nd on weekends. Minicab charges hould be negotiated in advance.

To book a black cab, call **Radio axis** (📞 **0207/272-0272**) or

Dial-a-Cab (📞 **0207/253-5000**). For a minicab, call **Addison Lee** (📞 **0207/387-8888**).

Fast Facts

PARTMENT RENTALS **Central London Apartments** (📞 **0845/644-2714**; www.central-london-apartments.com) offers serviced apartments in various locations throughout the city. **Home from Home** (📞 **0207/233-8111**; www.homefromhome.co.uk) has a good website that displays all kinds of apartments in numerous London neighborhoods.

TMs Called "Cashpoints" by the British, ATMs are everywhere, and most use global networks such as Cirrus and PLUS. Note that you may be charged a fee by your bank for withdrawing pounds from your foreign currency account.

ABYSITTING Reputable babysitting agencies with vetted employees include **Sitters** (📞 **0207/487-5040**; www.babysitter.co.uk) and **Universal Aunts** (📞 **0207/738-8937**). Rates run about £7 per hour during the day; £6 per hour in the evening. Hotel guests must pay a £10 booking fee and reasonable transportation costs.

&Bs **Bulldog Club,** 14 Dewhurst Rd. (📞 **0207/371-3202**; www.bulldogclub.com), and **Uptown Reservations** (📞 **0207/937-2001**; www.uptownres.co.uk) are two good reservation companies that offer lovely accommodations in private homes in good neighborhoods.

ANKING HOURS Most banks are open Monday through Friday from 9am to 5pm; some have limited Saturday open hours.

BIKE RENTALS **London Bicycle Tour Company,** Gabriel's Wharf, South Bank (📞 **0207/928-6838**; www.londonbicycle.com) rents a wide variety of bikes. Rates start at £3 per hour, and £18 per day, and £36 for 3 days.

BUSINESS HOURS Stores generally open at 10am and close around 6pm Monday through Saturday, though they may stay open until 7 or 8pm 1 night a week (usually Thurs). Some stores are open on Sunday from 11am or noon to 5pm. Post offices are open 9am to 5:30pm on weekdays.

CLIMATE See "Weather," later in this chapter.

CONSULATES & EMBASSIES **American Embassy,** 24 Grosvenor Sq. (📞 **0207/499-9000**; www.usembassy.org.uk). **Canadian High Commission,** 38 Grosvenor St. (📞 **0207/258-6600**; www.canada.org.uk). **Australian High Commission,** Australia House, Strand (📞 **0207/379-4334**; www.australia.org.uk). **Irish Embassy,** 17 Grosvenor Place (📞 **0207/235-7700**). **New Zealand High Commission,** New Zealand House, 80 Haymarket (📞 **0207/930-8422**; www.nzembassy.com).

CUSTOMS Check **www.hmce.gov.uk** for what foreign visitors may bring into London. For specifics on what you can bring home with you, Americans should consult the **U.S. Customs** website at www.customs.gov or call 📞 **202/354-1000**.

Canadians should contact the **Canadian Customs and Revenue Agency** (☎ 800/461-9999; www.ccra-adrc.gc.ca). Australians should contact **Australian Customs Services** (☎ 02/6275-6666; www.customs.gov.au). New Zealanders should contact **New Zealand Customs** (☎ 1800/428-786-60; www.customs.govt.nz).

DENTISTS **24 Hour Emergency Dental Treatment,** 102 Baker St. (☎ 0207/955-2186; www.24houremergencydentist.co.uk) delivers just what its name promises.

DINING Breakfasts range from the traditional meal of fried eggs, bacon, beans, grilled tomato, and toast to a more continental range of croissants, baguettes, and coffee. If your hotel doesn't include breakfast in its rates, breakfast in a cafe will likely be cheaper. Most cafes open from 8am to 8pm. Most restaurants open for lunch from noon to 3pm, and for dinner from 6 to 10 or 11pm. Dress codes have become much more relaxed, and except at very expensive restaurants and hotel dining rooms, no one will raise an eyebrow at casual clothing. You will encounter general disapproval if you bring small children to the nicer restaurants, especially at dinnertime.

Reservations at London's fanciest restaurants sometimes require bookings of up to 2 months in advance. Your best bet is to call the restaurant directly or reserve via its website. Many London restaurants take reservations via the Web through **www.toptable.co.uk**. You can also ask your hotel's concierge for help when you arrive or when you call to reserve your room.

DOCTORS A number of on-call doctor services can treat you and dispense medicine at your lodgings, or you can go to them. **Doctorcall,** 121 Harley St. (☎ 0700/037-2255;

www.doctorcall.co.uk), and **Pharmacentre,** 149 Edgeware Rd. (☎ 0808/208-5720; www.pharmacentre.co.uk), are in Central London and make house calls.

ELECTRICITY Britain uses a 220–240 volt system and alternating current (AC); its electrical plugs have three pins. European appliances will require only a plug adapter, but American 110-volt appliances will need both a transformer and an adapter or they will fry and blow a fuse. Most laptops have built-in electrical transformers, but will need an adapter plug.

EMERGENCIES Call ☎ 999 for accidents and dire medical emergencies free of charge from any phone. Hospitals with emergency rooms (known as Accident and Emergency departments, or A&E) in Central London include **Charing Cross Hospital,** Fulham Palace Road, Hammersmith (☎ 0208/846-1234); **Chelsea & Westminster Hospital,** Fulham Road, Chelsea (☎ 0208/746-8000); **St. Mary's Hospital,** Praed Street, Paddington (☎ 0207/886-6666); and **Guy's & St. Thomas's Hospital,** Lambeth Palace Road, Lambeth (☎ 0207/188-7188).

EVENT LISTINGS Good sources of event and entertainment listings include *Time Out,* the "Metro" section of Thursday's *Evening Standard*, *What's On,* and the Saturday and Sunday supplements in London's daily newspapers.

FAMILY TRAVEL Look for items tagged with a "kids" icon in this book. Most British hotels accommodate families all but the poshest restaurants are usually family-friendly. The London Tourist Board operates a kid-friendly website, **Kids Love London** (www.kidslovelondon.com), that provides information on family-friendly attractions, events, and restaurants, and offers discounts on various goods and services. For more detailed information, pick up *Frommer's London with Kids* (Wiley, Inc.) at your local bookstore.

GAY & LESBIAN TRAVELERS London has one of the most active lesbian and gay scenes in the world. The **London Lesbian & Gay Switchboard** (☎ 0207/837-7324; www.llgs.org.uk) provides advice on everything from gay-friendly lodging to entertainment.

HEALTH CLUBS Only expensive hotels have on-site health clubs, but many hotels have arrangements with nearby facilities that allow guests to use them for a fee. Unfortunately, because of the increase in injury suits, very few health clubs offer day passes anymore. **The Fitmap** (www.fitmap.co.uk) is a website that can steer you toward a nearby gym that might offer day passes to visitors.

HOLIDAYS Bank holidays, on which most shops and all banks, museums, public buildings, and services are closed, are as follows: New Year's Day, Good Friday (Fri before Easter), Easter Monday, May Day (first Mon in May), Spring Break (last Mon in May), Summer Break (last Mon in Aug), Christmas Day, and Boxing Day (Dec 26).

INSURANCE Check your existing insurance policies and credit card coverage before buying travel insurance. You may already be covered for lost luggage, canceled tickets, or medical expenses. If you aren't covered, expect to pay 5% to 8% of your trip's cost for insurance. For trip-cancellation and lost-luggage insurance, North Americans should try **Travel Guard International** (☎ 800/826-4919; www.travelguard.com) or **Travel Insured International** (☎ 800/243-3174; www.travelinsured.com). North Americans interested in getting medical insurance, including emergency evacuation coverage, can contact **Travel Assistance International**

(☎ 800/821-2828; www.travelassistance.com). U.K. travelers should contact **The Association of British Insurers** (☎ 0207/600-3333; www.abi.org.uk), which gives advice by phone and publishes *Holiday Insurance,* a free guide to policy provisions and prices. You might also shop around for better deals: Try **Columbus Direct** (☎ 0870/033-9988; www.columbusdirect.com).

INTERNET CAFES Almost every major street will have at least one cyber-cafe, either independently run or part of a chain; they are usually open from 9am to 11pm. To find a cafe near you, check **www.londononline.co.uk** and you'll find a long list, along with links for maps and directions.

LOST PROPERTY Be sure to tell all your credit card companies the minute you discover your wallet has been lost or stolen, and file a report at the nearest police precinct (your insurance company may require a police report before covering any claims). If you've lost all forms of photo ID, call your consulate and airline and explain the situation. It's always best to keep copies of your credit card numbers and passport information in a separate location in case you lose the real items.

For help in finding property lost on London public transport (buses, tube, and taxis), call the **TFL Lost Property Office,** 200 Baker St. (☎ 0845/330-9882); if you've lost something on an overground train, call the main terminal that serves the train on which you lost your property, or call the above number for help.

MAIL & POSTAGE Stamps for mail inside the U.K. cost 36p for first class and 27p for second class. Postage for postcards and letters sent outside the U.K. to Europe is 50p; postcards to the rest of the world cost 56p and letters are 81p. You can pay for and print out postage at **www.royalmail.com**, if you have a computer and printer. Most news agents carry stamps, and the city's distinctive red mailboxes are plentiful. The main post office in Trafalgar Square has the longest hours in London: 8:30am to 6:30pm Monday to Friday, and 9am to 5:30pm Saturday.

MONEY   England clings stubbornly to its pound sterling and pence. £1 consists of 100 pence (pennies). There are one- and two-pound coins; silvery 50p, 20p, 10p, and 5p coins; and copper 2p and 1p coins. Bank notes are issued in denominations of £50 (red), £20 (lavender), £10 (orange), and £5 (blue).

Foreign money can be exchanged at most banks and *bureaux de change,* but you'll be assessed a hefty surcharge or get terrible conversion rates. If you want to arrive with a few pounds in hand, get them from your bank before you leave home. ATMs (called Cashpoints) are located all over the city and offer the best exchange rates; find out your daily withdrawal limit before you leave home. At this writing, £1 was worth a hefty $2. For the most up-to-date currency conversion information, go to **www.xe.com**.

Many stores in London will not take traveler's checks, and those that do often charge stiff fees. It's best to stick to cash and credit cards, though most banks assess a 2% fee above the 1% fee charged by Visa, MasterCard, or American Express for currency conversions. Be sure to notify your credit card companies before leaving for London so they don't get become suspicious when the card is used numerous times in London and block your account.

PARKING   Parking in London is difficult, even for those who have paid for a resident parking permit (yet another reason I advise against renting a car here). Metered spaces have time limits of 1 to 4 hours and are hard to find.

Garages (car parks) are expensive, but plentiful. Look for signs that say **ncp** (for National Car Park); call ☎ **0845/050-7080** or check out **www.ncp.co.uk** for locations and more information.

Always check any yellow warning signs on streets for info on temporary parking suspensions. Parking violations are punished with a hefty fine, tire clamping, or the removal of your car to an impound lot. If your car has been towed, call ☎ **0207/747-4747**.

PASSES   There are two transport-plus-attraction-pass packages offered in London, and the websites are close enough in name to make it easy to confuse them. The site associated with Transport for London is at www.londontravelpass.com. Their prices for a travel-card-and-attraction-pass package are cheaper than those at the other site, www.londonpass.com. Both offer discounted travel and free admission to 55 of London's high-priced attractions, as well as other useful discounts.

The Transport for London Visitor Travelcard and London Pass Package prices are as follows: 1-day £37 adults, £20 kids; 3-day £50 adults, £24 kids; 7-day £93 adults, £55 kids. You don't need the London pass for most museums as they are free, but you will save money if you can cram a few fee-charging attractions into 1 or 3 days.

PASSPORTS   Citizens of the United States, Canada, Ireland, Australia, and New Zealand need only a valid passport to enter England. **U.S. residents** can download passport applications from the U.S. State Department website at http://travel.state.gov. Passport applications for **Canadian citizens** are available at local travel agencies and through the Passport Office, Department of Foreign Affairs and International Trade, Ottawa, ON K1A 0G3 (☎ **800/567-6868;** www.ppt.gc.ca). **Irish residents** can apply for a 10-year passport at the Passport Office, Setanta Centre, Molesworth Street, Dublin 2 (☎ **01/671-1633;** www.irlgov.ie/iveagh). **Australians** should contact the Australian Passport Information Service at ☎ **131-232,** or visit the government website at www.passports.gov.au. **New Zealand residents** can download applications from the Passports Office's website at www.passports.govt.nz.

Always make a copy of your passport's information page and keep it separate from your passport in case of loss or theft. For emergency passport replacement, contact your country's embassy or consulate (see "Consulates & Embassies," on p 161).

PHARMACIES These "chemists" can fill a valid doctor's prescription from home. One late-night pharmacy (open until midnight) is **Bliss Chemist,** 5–6 Marble Arch (☎ **0207/723-6116**). An all-night chemist is **Zafash Pharmacy,** 233–235 Old Brompton Rd., Earls Court (☎ **0207/373-2798**). The leading drugstore chain in the U.K., **Boots the Chemist** (www.boots.com), has branches all over London.

SAFETY London has its share of violent crime, just as any other major city does—its biggest crime-related problems are public intoxication, muggings, and rape—but it is usually quite safe for visitors as long as you take common-sense precautions. Good safety tips include:

- Use your hotel safe.
- Be alert when withdrawing money from ATMs; don't take out more cash than you need, and don't carry large sums around.
- Guard your valuables in public places and keep your wallet in an inner pocket. Pickpockets operate in all the major tourist zones.
- Don't leave pocketbooks dangling from chairs in restaurants or Internet cafes; use a purse that closes securely.
- Avoid conspicuous displays of expensive jewelry.
- Avoid the upper decks of buses late at night. Take a cab if you can afford it.
- Stay alert in high-end shopping areas: Bags from luxury shops are a tip-off to thieves.
- There's safety in numbers—don't wander alone in Soho or the West End late at night. And stay out of parks after dark.
- Don't hop in a minicab hailed off the street. Stick to official black cabs.

SENIOR TRAVELERS Discounts (concessions) for seniors over 64 are available (with proof of age) for museums and some entertainment. **Elderhostel** (☎ **800/454-5768** in the U.S.; www.elderhostel.org) organizes well-priced "study trips" to many world destinations, including London; the courses are geared toward active seniors, and accommodations may be spartan.

SMOKING Smoking is prohibited in shops, on all public transportation, and inside Tube stations. As of July 2007, all public buildings, restaurants, pubs, and bars are strictly nonsmoking. Tobacco is expensive in the U.K., so if you smoke, bring your cigarettes from home or buy them in the airport duty-free shop.

The Savvy Traveler

SPECTATOR SPORTS London is crazy for football (that's soccer to you Americans out there) and is home to three professional teams. The best place to watch the English lose their decorum in the stands is the **Chelsea Club,** Stamford Bridge, Fulham Road (☎ **0870/300-2322;** www.chelseafc.com). Wear blue and you'll fit right in. For a more genteel (albeit confusing) experience, try watching a cricket match at the sport's most hallowed field—**Lords Cricket Club,** St. John's Wood Road (☎ **0207/616-8500;** www.lords.org).

The most sacred annual London sporting event is June's **Lawn Tennis Championships at Wimbledon** (☎ **0208/971-2473** for tickets, 0208/944-1066 for information; www.wimbledon.com). Check the website for details on how to enter your name for the January lottery tickets. Same-day seats to the outside courts are available, but you'll wait in very long lines.

TAXES A 17.5% value-added tax (VAT) is assessed on hotel and restaurant bills, merchandise, and most services. Non-E.U. visitors are eligible for partial VAT refunds (for more information, see p 77). Note that price tags on items in stores already include the VAT (except in some antique shops). Gasoline (petrol) in Britain is taxed at 25%.

TAXIS See "By Taxi," on p 160.

TELEPHONES London has three types of public pay phones: those accepting only coins, those accepting only phone cards (Cardphones), and those that take both phone cards and most major credit cards. Phone cards can be purchased in several denominations (£2–£20) at most newsstands and post offices. The minimum charge for a local call is 40p.

London's city code is **020,** but you don't need to dial it within city limits; just dial the eight-digit number. To call London from the rest of

the U.K., you must dial the 020 followed by the number. When calling London from abroad, dial the international code (011 from North America; 0011 from Australia; and 00 from New Zealand), followed by 44 (England's country code), followed by 20, and then the eight-digit number.

When calling abroad from London, dial 00, the country code, the area code, and then the number. Directory assistance in London can be reached by calling ☎ **118 180,** but try to dial numbers direct, because connection costs through directory assistance companies are high.

TICKETS Most West End theaters keep a few seats in reserve to sell on the day of a performance. If you're set on seeing a specific show or event (especially the ballet or opera), book your tickets in advance (for a small service fee) through **Londontown** (www.londontown. com), **Ticketmaster** (www.ticket master.co.uk), or **Keith Prowse** (www.keithprowse.com). You can also try calling the box office directly.

You can get half-price theater tickets at the free-standing kiosk on the south side of Leicester Square for same-day performances of selected shows. For more information on buying tickets in advance, see p 135.

TIPPING Check restaurant bills for an automatic service charge, which usually runs around 12% to 15%. If service hasn't been included, tip your waiter 15%. Tip taxi drivers, hairdressers, and bartenders 10% to 15%. It is not usual to tip hotel chambermaids, though you may certainly do so. Hotel porters should get £1 per bag; doormen should get £1 for hailing you a cab. You aren't expected to tip at a pub unless table service is provided.

TOILETS Clean, city-maintained public toilets can be found in shopping areas, parks, and tourist zones. Some are free, and some charge either 20p or 50p for use. Pubs and hotels don't get too fussy if you discreetly nip in to use the loo (especially if you buy a drink first). Department stores have public restrooms, usually stashed on high floors to discourage traffic. For more information on public restrooms, see p 63.

TOURIST OFFICES Drop into the official **London Tourist Board Visitor Centre,** 1 Lower Regent St. (☎ **0207/808-3800;** www.visit london.com; Tube: Piccadilly Circus), for information in eight languages, useful pamphlets, maps, Travelcards, and souvenirs. The center also has a decent cafe and offers currency exchange and Internet access. It's open 9am to 6:30pm weekdays, and 10am to 4pm weekends.

TOURIST TRAPS & SCAMS Madame Tussaud's Wax Museum is London's most puzzlingly popular tourist trap—it's crowded, it's outrageously expensive, and it offers little cultural value. The half-price theater-ticket shops around Soho are rip-offs (they tag on a heavy commission for poor seats), and most tickets sold on the street are counterfeit; use only the official half-price ticket booth at the south end of Leicester Square. Forget the street peddlers selling perfume and accessories. See "Safety," above.

TOURS Two similar companies offer good orientation tours of the city from the vantage of a double-decker bus: **London Big Bus** (☎ **0800/ 169-1365;** www.bigbus.co.uk) and **Original London Sightseeing Tour** (☎ **0208/877-1722;** www.the originaltour.com). Tickets, good for 24 hours, allow visitors to hop on and off buses that stop at most of Central London's major attractions

(buses run every 15–30 min.). Both companies' tours take about 2 hours; audio commentary is available in a number of languages. The Big Bus tour ticket also covers a small selection of themed walking tours.

Black Taxi Tours of London (☎ **0207/935-9363;** www.blacktaxi tours.co.uk) offers personalized 2-hour tours in a genuine black cab for up to five people for £90. The cabs can venture where buses cannot, making it easier to get off the tourist trail.

For walking tours of London that are geared to particular interests or themes, you can't do better than **The Original London Walks** (☎ **0207/624-3978;** www.walks. com). Expert guides lead visitors on tours ranging from ghost walks to strolls through literary London to historic pub crawls.

If you want to tour London via the Thames, **City Cruises** (☎ **0207/ 740-0400;** www.citycruises.com) runs sightseeing trips in modern riverboats equipped with audio commentary in six languages. Tours depart from Westminster, Waterloo, and Tower piers; they range in duration from 30 minutes to 2½ hours.

Many of the city's museums and royal palaces offer daily gallery talks and themed tours inspired by the various objects in their collections.

TRAVELERS WITH DISABILITIES Most of London's major museums are fitted with wheelchair ramps. Discounts for travelers with disabilities, known as "concessions," are offered by many attractions and theaters. **Holiday Care Services** (☎ **0845/ 124-9971;** www.holidaycare.org.uk) offers loads of information and advice for travelers with disabilities visiting Britain. Visitors with disabilities planning to travel via public transportation should order *Access* *in London,* an essential guide for travelers with disabilities, put out by **Artsline;** it can be ordered at **www.accessinlondon.org.**

VAT   See "Taxes," above.

WEATHER   For the local London forecast, call ☎ **0906/823-2771;** or go to **www.weather.com** for up-to-date weather information.

A Brief **History**

A.D. 43   Romans invade England and settle Londinium.

A.D. 61   Queen Boadicea sacks Londinium in a brutal but unsuccessful rebellion against Rome.

200   Romans fortify the city with a wall.

400   Roman troops abandon London as the Empire falls.

600   King Ethelbert builds first St. Paul's Church on ruins of Temple of Diana.

800   Vikings raid Britain.

885   Alfred the Great captures London from the Vikings.

1042   Edward the Confessor is crowned king of England and begins work on Westminster Abbey.

1066   William the Conqueror is crowned king of England in Westminster Abbey after the Battle of Hastings. London becomes seat of political power.

1078   Construction of the Tower of London begins.

1176–1209   London Bridge is built, connecting the two banks of the Thames.

1192   Henry FitzAilwin is elected first lord mayor of London.

1215   Magna Carta is signed by King John.

1240   First Parliament is convened at Westminster.

1348   First outbreak of the Black Death plagues London.

1381   Wat Tyler's Peasant Revolt is mercilessly crushed.

1476   William Caxton, the first English printer, revolutionizes London and makes Fleet Street the country's publishing center.

1509   Henry VIII ascends the throne.

1534–36   Henry VIII breaks with Rome and establishes the Church of England, an action leading to the Dissolution of the Monasteries.

1553–58   Catholic Queen Mary I executes thousands of Protestants, earning the nickname "Bloody Mary."

1558   Elizabeth I is crowned.

1588   Spanish Armada is defeated.

1599   Shakespeare's first play is performed at the Globe Theatre.

1605   Guy Fawkes's November 5 Gunpowder Plot to destroy Parliament is thwarted.

1642–58   English Civil War pits Royalists against Parliamentarians.

1649   Charles I is beheaded at Whitehall.

1653   Oliver Cromwell is made Lord Protector of the Realm. Puritan rule closes London's theaters, brothels, and gaming halls.

1660 Charles II is brought back from exile in France and the monarchy is restored.

1665 Outbreak of bubonic plague kills 100,000 Londoners.

1666 Great Fire of London sweeps through the city.

1667 Christopher Wren begins work on St. Paul's Cathedral; attempts to redraw London's map are abandoned.

1688 James II is banished during the Bloodless Revolution; William and Mary move into Kensington Palace.

1694 First Bank of England is established.

1735 Dr. Samuel Johnson moves to London and becomes a fixture on the coffeehouse circuit.

1759 The British Museum is opened to the public.

1829 Robert Peel sets up Metropolitan Police force, known as "bobbies" in his honor.

1836 Charles Dickens publishes *The Pickwick Papers* and becomes London's favorite novelist.

1837 Eighteen-year-old Queen Victoria ascends the throne and moves into Buckingham Palace.

1851 Great Exhibition takes place in Hyde Park, financing the development of South Kensington.

1854 Cholera epidemic in London results in improved sewage system.

1857 Victoria and Albert Museum opens.

1860 London's first public flushing toilet opens.

1863 London opens the world's first Underground Transit System.

1901 Queen Victoria dies; Edward VI is crowned.

1914 World War I starts; zeppelins drop bombs on London.

1936 King Edward VIII abdicates throne to marry American divorcée Wallis Simpson.

1939–45 World War II air raids kill thousands in London and destroy much of the city's infrastructure.

1953 Queen Elizabeth II is crowned.

1963 Youth-quake in London: The Beatles and the Rolling Stones rule the day.

1970s Irish Republican Army engages in terrorist bomb offensive.

1979 Margaret Thatcher becomes Britain's first female prime minister.

1981 Prince Charles marries Lady Diana Spencer in St. Paul's Cathedral.

1994 Channel Tunnel opens.

1997 Tony Blair becomes prime minister of Britain; London mourns the death of Princess Diana.

2000 Traditional pigeon feeding in Trafalgar Square is outlawed.

2002 London celebrates Elizabeth II's Golden Jubilee.

2005 London wins bid for the 2012 Olympics; 55 die in terrorist attack on London transport.

2008 The Labour Party heads into troubled times as Gordon Brown takes over from Tony Blair.

London's **Architecture**

Norman Period: 1066–1200
The oldest surviving style of architecture in London dates back to the time of William the Conqueror, when the Normans overran England. Thick walls and masonry were used to support the large interiors needed to accommodate the churchgoing masses. The heavy construction usually gave Norman buildings a dark and foreboding air.

Characteristics of the period include:

- Thick walls with small windows
- Round weight-bearing arches
- Huge piers (square stacks of masonry)
- Chevrons—zigzagging decorations surrounding doorways or wrapped around columns

White Tower.

The Tower of London's **White Tower,** built by William the Conqueror, is a textbook example of a Norman-style castle. **St. John's Chapel** within the White Tower is one of the few remaining Norman-style churches in England.

Gothic: 1150–1550
French in origin, the fairy-tale Gothic style introduced innovations that allowed builders to transfer weight away from a structure's walls so they could be taller and thinner. The style also allowed for the use of larger windows, which allowed more natural light to reach a building's interior.

In addition to the pointed arch, Gothic construction features:

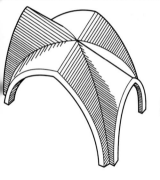

Cross Vault.

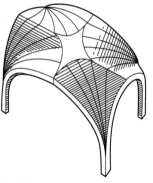

Fan Vault.

- Vaulted ceilings, using cross vaulting (an "X" design) and fan vaulting (a more conic design)
- Flying buttresses, free-standing exterior pillars that helped support the buildings' weight
- Carved tracery stonework connecting windows
- Stained-glass windows

You need look no further than **Westminster Abbey,** built in the mid–14th century, for a perfect London example of the Gothic style.

Renaissance: 1550–1650
The Renaissance style, involving proportion and mathematical precision

enlivened by decoration, was imported from the Continent by the great Inigo Jones, who was greatly influenced by Italian Palladianism.

Characteristics of Renaissance architecture include:

- A sense of proportion
- A reliance on symmetry
- The use of classical columns—Doric, Ionic, and Corinthian

Top examples of this style include the **Banqueting Hall at Whitehall** and the **arcade** of Covent Garden, both designed by Inigo Jones.

Classical Orders.

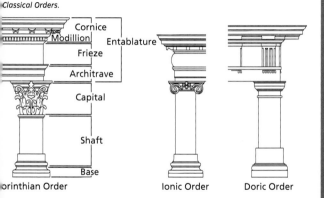

Corinthian Order   Ionic Order   Doric Order

Baroque: 1650–1750

Baroque architects Christopher Wren and Nicholas Hawksmoor had unrivalled opportunities to practice their craft in London when the Great Fire of 1666 provided a clean palette on which to replace medieval wooden structures.

The prime features of the more fanciful baroque style include:

- Classical forms marked by grand curving lines
- Decoration with playful carvings

St. Paul's Cathedral, with its massive dome and complex exterior decor, is Wren's crowning achievement and the finest example of English baroque architecture in London.

Neoclassical & Greek Revival: 1714–1837

Neoclassicism was an 18th-century reaction to the busy nature of baroque architecture. Notable characteristics of neoclassical architecture include:

- Clean, elegant lines, with balance and symmetry
- Use of classical Greek columns
- Crescent layouts (half-circles of identical stone houses with tall windows)

Sir John Soane's Museum, and John Nash's curving white stucco **Cumberland Terrace** in Regent's Park, are exemplars of these styles.

Victorian Gothic Revival: 1750–1900

As industrialism began its inexorable march on London, artists and architects looked back to a simpler and more romantic fairy-tale period for their inspiration.

The features that marked the Gothic Revival style include:

St. Paul's Cathedral.

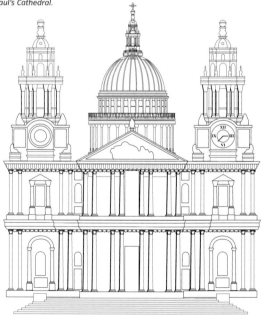

Palace of Westminster.

- A confusion of spires, arches, and decorative detail
- Buildings constructed on a grand scale

The **Palace of Westminster,** home to the British Parliament, is the farthest-reaching exponent of this style; the most compact is the **Albert Memorial** in Hyde Park.

20th & Early 21st Century: 1900–Present

The 20th century saw London expanding into its suburbs with uninspired architecture. The Blitz was the period's (far more tragic) version of the Great Fire, and the rebuilding took place with postwar austerity. The ugly, utilitarian style of South Bank's **Royal Festival Hall** is known as **Brutalism. Post-modernism** is a softening of that style, applying the whimsy of the past to the modern, which brought about the inside-out **Lloyd's Building,** and the **Gherkin Building.** The best marriage of old and new can be seen in the covered **Great Court** of the British Museum, which managed to put a new hat on an old friend without making it look silly.

The Wren Style

One of the great geniuses of his age (and London's greatest architect), Sir Christopher Wren (1632–1723) was a professor of astronomy at Oxford before becoming an architect. After the Great Fire of London in 1666, Wren was chosen to rebuild the devastated city and its many churches, including St. Paul's, on which work began in 1675. His designs had great originality, and he became known for his spatial effects and his impressive fusion of classical and baroque. He believed in classical stability and repose, yet he liked to enliven his churches with baroque whimsy and fantasy. Nothing better represents the Wren style than the facade of St. Paul's (p 13, ⑪), for which he combined classical columns, reminiscent of Greek temples, with baroque decorations and adornments.

Toll-Free Numbers & Websites

Airlines

AER LINGUS
☎ 800/474-7424 in the U.S.
☎ 01/886-8888 in Ireland
www.aerlingus.com

AIR CANADA
☎ 888/247-2262
www.aircanada.ca

AIR NEW ZEALAND
☎ 0800/737-767 in New Zealand
www.airnewzealand.com

AMERICAN AIRLINES
☎ 800/433-7300
www.aa.com

BRITISH AIRWAYS
☎ 800/247-9297
☎ 0845/773-3377 in Britain
www.british-airways.com

CONTINENTAL AIRLINES
☎ 800/525-0280
www.continental.com

DELTA AIR LINES
☎ 800/221-1212
www.delta.com

EASYJET
No number.
www.easyjet.com

NORTHWEST AIRLINES
☎ 800/225-2525
www.nwa.com

QANTAS
☎ 800/227-4500 in the U.S.
☎ 13 13 13 in Australia
www.qantas.com

RYANAIR
☎ 0818 30 30 30 in Ireland
☎ 0871/246-0000 in the U.K.
☎ 01 353 1 249 7700 for the U.S.
www.ryanair.com

UNITED AIRLINES
☎ 800/241-6522
www.united.com

US AIRWAYS
☎ 800/428-4322
www.usairways.com

VIRGIN ATLANTIC AIRWAYS
☎ 800/862-8621 in the U.S.
☎ 0870/380-2007 in Britain
www.virgin-atlantic.com

Car Rental Agencies

ALAMO
☎ 800/327-9633
www.goalamo.com

AUTO EUROPE
☎ 800/223-5555
www.autoeurope.com

AVIS
☎ 800/331-1212 in the U.S.
☎ 800/TRY-AVIS in Canada
www.avis.com

BUDGET
☎ 800/527-0700
www.budget.com

DOLLAR
☎ 800/800-4000
www.dollar.com

ENTERPRISE
☎ 800/325-8007
www.enterprise.com

HERTZ
☎ 800/654-3131
www.hertz.com

KEMWEL HOLIDAY AUTO
☎ 800/678-0678 or 877/820-0668
www.kemwel.com

NATIONAL
☎ 800/CAR-RENT
www.nationalcar.com

THRIFTY
☎ 800/367-2277
www.thrifty.com

Major Hotel & Motel Chains

BEST WESTERN INTERNATIONAL
☎ 800/528-1234
www.bestwestern.com

COMFORT INNS
☎ 800/228-5150
www.hotelchoice.com

CROWNE PLAZA HOTELS
☎ 888/303-1746
www.crowneplaza.com

DAYS INN
☎ 800/325-2525
www.daysinn.com

HILTON HOTELS
☎ 800/HILTONS
www.hilton.com

HOLIDAY INN
☎ 800/HOLIDAY
www.ichotelsgroup.com

HYATT HOTELS & RESORTS
☎ 800/228-9000
www.hyatt.com

INTER-CONTINENTAL HOTELS & RESORTS
☎ 888/567-8725
www.ichotelsgroup.com

RADISSON HOTELS INTERNATIONAL
☎ 800/333-3333
www.radisson.com

RED CARNATION HOTELS
☎ 877/955-1515
www.redcarnationhotels.com

SHERATON HOTELS & RESORTS
☎ 800/325-3535
www.sheraton.com

THISTLE HOTELS
☎ 0870/333-9292
www.thistlehotels.com

Index

Photo **Credits**